CW00408069

WEAPONS, WIRELESS
and WORLD WARS

First published in 2010 by Libri Publishing

Copyright © Jim Lewis

ISBN 978 1 907471 00 1

All rights reserved. No part of this publication may be reproduced, stored in any retrieval system or transmitted in any form or by any means, electronic, mechanical, photocopying, recording or otherwise, without the prior written permission of the copyright holder for which application should be addressed in the first instance to the publishers. No liability shall be attached to the author, the copyright holder or the publishers for loss or damage of any nature suffered as a result of reliance on the reproduction of any of the contents of this publication or any errors or omissions in its contents.

A CIP catalogue record for this book is available from The British Library

Design by Helen Taylor

Maps by Alice Gadney of Silver7 Mapping Ltd

Printed in the UK by Ashford Colour Press

Libri Publishing
Brunel House
Volunteer Way
Faringdon
Oxfordshire
SN7 7YR

Tel: +44 (0)845 873 3837
www.libripublishing.co.uk

WEAPONS, WIRELESS and WORLD WARS

the vital role of the Lea Valley

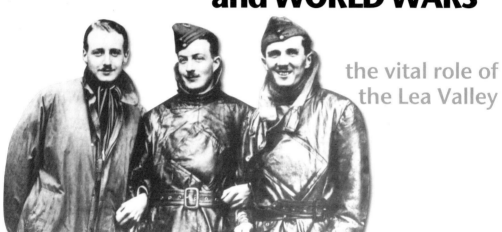

Jim Lewis

LIBRI
PUBLISHING

Aerial view of the Johnson Matthey plant at Brimsdown, Enfield.

SPONSOR PROFILE

Libri Publishing was supported in the publication of this book by Johnson Matthey.

As a company which can trace its Lea Valley roots to the early-20th century we have pleasure in sponsoring this book in Jim Lewis's new Lea Valley series.

Johnson Matthey, has, over the years, developed and supplied specialist materials that have been used by many industries not only to enhance the quality of life of millions around the world but also to be used in the quest to secure peace. For example, precious metals like platinum, used in the manufacture of electrical contacts, have contributed to the quality and reliability of a wide range of electronic communications equipment used by the military. Platinum group metals produced by Johnson Matthey were also used in key components for aircraft engines and in radar equipment during the Second World War.

It was a quirk of fate at the time of the Great War that eventually brought Johnson Matthey to Brimsdown in London's Lea Valley. Johnson and Sons, a company established by John Johnson, the father of Percival Norton Johnson, Johnson Matthey's founder, and run by the descendants of P.N. Johnson's brothers, had three businesses: smelting, assaying and manufacturing chemists. After the death of John Grove Johnson in 1908, the smelting side of the business, which was then in Paul Street, in the City of London, was taken over by his daughter Edith. At the time the work mainly consisted of refining gold dust, amalgam, silver derivatives and also the sweepings from various jewellers and craft workshops. At the outbreak of war in 1914, the shipment of bullion and other precious metals to Britain all but dried up because of the risk of capture or loss through enemy action.

Arthur B. Stuart, who had taken over the running of the Paul Street smelting facility, was desperate to secure new business to stop Johnson and Sons Smelting Works going under. He approached the government for help and was fortunate in securing a contract for the south of England to smelt copper scrap, the waste product of wartime shell factories. The purified material was turned into Best Selected Copper that was used by the Royal Mint and also in the production of munitions. The contract was largely responsible for keeping the company afloat throughout the war years.

At the cessation of hostilities Johnson and Sons once again began refining gold bullion. However, due to the wartime policy of not shipping the material, stocks in South Africa had built up and the African gold-mining companies had had little alternative but to begin their own refining. As might be imagined, the initiative proved disastrous for the Company's Paul Street Works and Arthur Stuart was again faced with the task of saving the business. Coincidentally the skills of smelting copper scrap, learned during the war years, was to throw a lifeline to the firm. Stuart now turned to the base-metal industries for contracts and took on the work of smelting their by-products. Johnson and Sons' war work in copper scrap smelting had produced hundred of tons of copper-rich slag and the decision was taken to process this waste material. While the idea in itself seemed sound, it was obvious that the capacity of the Paul Street Works was insufficient for the task and a new site would have to be found.

After rejecting several sites close to central London, Stuart, who was living near the Sewardstone Road, on the Essex side of the Lea Valley, came up with an inspirational idea. From the slightly elevated position of his house he could see the disused gravel workings on the other side of the valley. While unattractive to many, the Brimsdown site with its water-filled gravel pits provided the ideal solution to Stuart's quest for expansion. He reasoned that the pits could be used to store the left-over solid waste after smelting the copper slag. Also the nearby railway would offer a convenient transport link for moving product. The site, bounded by the Lee Navigation to the east and Mossops Creek to the north, was purchased and by 1922 a number of huts had been erected to provide office and processing space.

Johnson & Sons (assayers) carried on at their Paul Street address while Brimsdown was being established and the other branch of the company, Johnson & Sons, Manufacturing Chemists, maintained their business interests at Hendon, north London. However, by the mid-1920s the London Gold Market was in decline and the British economy was heading towards a serious downturn. Faced with the rapidly declining market conditions Stuart was again forced to look for a rescue strategy for the assaying and bullion smelting business as contracts began to dry up.

The most natural place to look for assistance was to their strong competitor and by now distant relations, Johnson Matthey & Company. As luck would have it, Johnson Matthey's own smelting operations at Patricroft, near Manchester, were in need of urgent modernisation. Stuart was able to strike a deal and in 1926 Johnson Matthey acquired the entire shareholding of Johnson and Sons' assaying and smelting businesses and proceeded to expand the Brimsdown plant.

So, conditions after the Great War provided the impetus which eventually led to the establishment of Johnson Matthey at Brimsdown in London's Lea Valley from where its Catalysts, Chemicals and Refining business continues to operate.

Today Johnson Matthey is a FTSE 100 speciality chemicals company focused on its core skills in catalysis, precious metals, fine chemicals and process technology. Its principal activities are the manufacture of autocatalysts, heavy duty diesel catalysts and pollution control systems, catalysts and components for fuel cells, catalysts and technologies for chemical processes, fine chemicals, chemical catalysts and active pharmaceutical ingredients and the marketing, refining, and fabrication of precious metals.

Johnson Matthey has operations in over 30 countries and employs around 8,500 people. Its products are sold across the world to a wide range of advanced technology industries.

Johnson Matthey

DEDICATION

This book is dedicated to my family and also to
my late mother and father, Leonora Maud Lewis
and Walter Harry Portman Lewis.

ABOUT THE AUTHOR

Dr Jim Lewis has spent most of his career in the consumer electronics industry, apart from a three-year spell in the Royal Air Force servicing airborne and ground wireless communications equipment. When working in the Lea Valley for Thorn EMI Ferguson he represented the company abroad on several occasions and was involved in the exchange of manufacturing technology. Currently he is a Consultant to Terry Farrell & Partners on the historical development of London's Lea Valley and a Workers' Educational Association (WEA) tutor teaching industrial history. He also teaches students within the Community Programme who have learning difficulties. A freelance writer, researcher and broadcaster for his specialist subject – London's Lea Valley – he also has a genuine passion for encouraging partnership projects within the local community, which in the long term are planned to help stimulate social and economic regeneration. Dr Lewis is married with four grown-up children and lives in Lincolnshire.

The author Dr Jim Lewis cutting the ribbon, with the Director of the Pump House Steam & Transport Museum Trust, Lindsay Collier MA, to open a special exhibition commemorating the 90th anniversary of the birth of the Associated Equipment Company (AEC), Walthamstow, the company responsible for the founding of London Transport (now Transport for London). Lindsay Collier and the Pump House Steam & Transport Museum Trust are responsible for designing and promoting the *Lea Valley Experience* project.

SERIES ACKNOWLEDGEMENTS

The author wishes to thank the following organisations, companies and societies for their encouragement, support and advice and for supplying many of the illustrations within this book:

Alexandra Palace and Park Trust, Wood Green, London
BAE Systems, Farnborough, Hampshire
Bishopsgate Institute, London
Black & Ethnic Minority Business Association, Walthamstow, London
BOC Process Plants, Edmonton, London
Brooklands Museum, Weybridge, Surrey
Bruce Castle Museum, Tottenham, London
Civix, Exton Street, London
Corporation of Trinity House, Tower Hill, London
Cuffley Industrial Heritage Society, Cuffley, Hertfordshire
Edmonton Hundred Historical Society, Enfield, Middlesex
Enfield Archaeological Society, Enfield, Middlesex
Enfield Business Centre, Enfield, Middlesex
Enfield Energy Centre Limited, Enfield, Middlesex
Enfield Enterprise Agency, Enfield, Middlesex
Enfield Local History Unit, Enfield, Middlesex
English Heritage, Blandford Street, London
Epping Forest Museum, Waltham Abbey, Essex
Greater London Record Office, Northampton Road, London
Gunpowder Mills Study Group, Guildford, Surrey
Guy & Wright Ltd., Green Tye, Hertfordshire
Hackney Society, Hackney, London
Harper Collins Publishers, Hammersmith, London
Hawker Siddeley Power Transformers, Walthamstow, London
Historical Publications Ltd., Barnsbury, London
Hornsey Historical Society, Hornsey, London
House of Lords Record Office, Westminster, London
Imperial War Museum, Duxford, Cambridgeshire
Institution of Civil Engineers, George Street, London
Institution of Engineering and Technology, Savoy Place, London
Institution of Mechanical Engineers, Birdcage Walk, London
Jewish Museum, Finchley, London
John Higgs, Freelance Historian, Fairford, Gloucestershire
Johnson Matthey, Enfield, Middlesex
Lea Valley Growers Association, Cheshunt, Hertfordshire
Lee Valley Business and Innovation Centre, Enfield, Middlesex
Lee Valley Regional Park Authority, Enfield, Middlesex
London Borough of Enfield, Enfield, Middlesex
London Borough of Haringey, Haringey, London
London Borough of Newham, East Ham, London
London Borough of Waltham Forest, Walthamstow, London
London Lee Valley Partnership Limited, Great Eastern Street, London
London Organising Committee of the Olympic & Paralympic Games, Canary Wharf, London
London Waste Ltd, Edmonton, London
Lotus Engineering, Hethel, Norwich, Norfolk
Marconi Archive, Oxford University Library Services, Oxford, Oxfordshire

Markfield Beam Engine & Museum, Tottenham, London
Midland Publishing Limited, Earl Shilton, Leicester
Ministry of Defence Library, Royal Armouries, Leeds, Yorkshire
Museum of London, London Wall, London
National Archive, Kew, Richmond, Surrey
National Army Museum, Chelsea, London
National Maritime Museum, Greenwich, London
National Portrait Gallery, London
Natural History Museum, Kensington, London
Navtech Systems Ltd., Market Harborough, Leicestershire
New River Action Group, Hornsey, London
Newham Local History Library, Stratford, London
North London Strategic Alliance, Wood Green, London
Perkins Group, Leyton, London
Phillips Auctioneers & Valuers, New Bond Street, London
Potters Bar Historical Society, Potters Bar, Hertfordshire
Pump House Steam & Transport Museum, Walthamstow, London
RCHME Cambridge, (National Monuments Record), Cambridge, Cambridgeshire
Reuters Limited, Fleet Street, London
River Lea Tidal Mill Trust, Bromley-by-Bow, London
Royal Air Force Museum, Hendon, London
Royal Commission on Historic Manuscripts, Quality Court, Chancery Lane, London
Royal Society of Chemistry, Burlington House, London
Royal Television Society, Holborn Hall, London
Science Museum, Kensington, London
Scout Association, Chingford, Essex
Southgate District Civic Trust, Southgate, London
Speedway Museum, Broxbourne, Hertfordshire
Stratford City Challenge, Stratford, London
Tesco, Cheshunt, Hertfordshire
Thames Water, Reading, Berkshire
Thorn EMI Archive, Hayes, Middlesex
Tower Hamlets Local History Library, Tower Hamlets, London
University of Leicester Space Research Group, Leicester, Leicestershire
Upper Lee Valley Partnership, Tottenham Hale, London
Valley Grown Nurseries, Nazeing, Essex
Vauxhall Heritage, Luton, Bedfordshire
Eric Verdon-Roe, grandson of Alliott Verdon-Roe
Vestry House Museum, Walthamstow, London
Waltham Abbey Royal Gunpowder Mills Company Ltd., Waltham Abbey, Essex
Walthamstow Amateur Cine Video Club, Walthamstow, London
WEA, London District, Luke Street, London
Wordsworth Editions, Ware, Hertfordshire

While many individuals have freely given their knowledge, some unknowingly, which has contributed greatly to the production of this series of books, I have, on a number of occasions paid special tribute to certain people in the footnotes of various chapters.

I could not let the occasion pass without recording my sincere thanks to my wife Jenny for her superb editorial skills and outstanding patience. The author freely admits that this voluntary sacrifice on Jenny's part has comprehensively tested the cement that holds our wonderful marriage together.

AUTHOR'S NOTE

Events such as the Olympics can be brought into our homes and workplaces from the host country as they take place through the power of electronic communication – radio, television, the Internet and satellite broadcasts. The technology that allowed this to happen was first discovered and developed at Ponders End, Enfield in London's Lea Valley.

In November 1904, after much experiment, Professor Ambrose Fleming registered his patent for the diode valve, the world's first thermionic device. This inspired invention not only paved the way for today's multimedia electronics industry, but also created the delivery platform for space travel, e-mail and the Internet, not to mention computers.

Thirty-two years after Fleming's invention, in November 1936, the world's first high-definition public service television broadcasts were transmitted by the BBC from Alexandra Palace, positioned on the crest of the Lea Valley's western slopes.

Centring the 2012 Olympic and Paralympic Games in London's Lea Valley will provide a unique opportunity to remind the world that it was the development of electronic communication within the region that has allowed the participating nations to share the message of peace and friendship.

Jim Lewis

CONTENTS

INTRODUCTION

I t is probably fair to say that authors who research interesting and little-known historical subjects tend to resist the requests of their readers to produce yet another book highlighting new facts. Then, as in my case, the pressure becomes too great and the research bullet has to be bitten. Once the decision is made there is no turning back and the author is faced with months, sometimes years, of archive research to follow up reader leads and to see if sufficient material exists in a particular subject area to construct an interesting and worthwhile story. While the prospect of the challenge at first may appear daunting, once fully committed and immersed in the work the excitement level builds and it is particularly satisfying when new information comes to light.

In my last three books, I invited readers, particularly teachers and school children, to get involved in Lea Valley projects and also to take on the role of detectives to discover if more interesting stories existed about the region. Some schools and universities rose to the challenge and on a number of occasions I was invited to become involved and also to act as a Lea Valley tour guide. It is occasions like these that make writing doubly rewarding.

Due to considerable local interest, and also the requests by many retailers for reprints of earlier material, the author has been persuaded to deviate from the intentions of the original format used in my earlier Lea Valley books, that of keeping chapters deliberately short, and for this new series I shall include a fuller treatment of many of the subjects. Therefore, it is intended to give each book in the series a particular theme. In this way it is hoped that that the readers' requests will be largely satisfied and also a greater insight into the developments of the region will be achieved.

I have been greatly encouraged to be quoted by prominent writers and broadcasters such as Ian Sinclair and also to receive letters from Dr Adam Hart-Davis saying "I had no idea that the great George Parker Bidder was, no less, 'the maker of modern West Ham'. I told the story in the wilds of Moretonhampstead."The BBC newscaster Mike Embly, once referred to me as the "Lea Valley alarm clock" as

I appear to wake people up to the historic significance of the region. These compliments make the long hours in front of a computer screen and the many years of archive research seem worthwhile and this encourages me to discover and write more about the Lea Valley, its entrepreneurs and its world firsts. Perhaps, sometime in the future the region will no longer be Britain's best-kept secret.

As I am mindful that the forthcoming Olympics will bring many people to the Lea Valley from around the world, who will want to learn a little more about the region, I have decided to include some stories to attract those readers with broader interests beyond that of the subject of industrial heritage.

Jim Lewis

1. THE FIRST WAR IN THE AIR

The Great War (1914–18) completely changed the way subsequent wars would be fought. The deliberate targeting of the civilian population in Britain opened up a new chapter of warfare with a strategy that was both inhumane and ruthless. This was not just about the death of innocent people and the destruction of property; it was also an attempt to create fear, heighten anxiety and lower morale. It was a new tactic to increase the psychological pressure on vulnerable people at home in the hope of destroying the determination of a nation to overcome the threats of an aggressor.

THE WORLD'S FIRST BLITZ
Many people believe that the world's first Blitz was the German bombing of London and other major UK targets during the Second World War, which engaged the Royal Air Force fighter squadrons in the Battle of Britain, but nothing could be further from the truth. In fact, some of the most dramatic aerial encounters of the Great War occurred in Lea Valley air space.

The first Blitz began on 19 January 1915 when two German Zeppelins dropped 24 50kg high-explosive and a number of 3kg incendiary bombs on the Norfolk towns of Great Yarmouth, King's Lynn and Sheringham, with some of the missiles falling on surrounding villages. As a result, four people were killed and a further 16 injured, with property damage estimated to be almost £7,500. This is the first time in history that civilians were deliberately killed by an enemy air strike. An additional 19 air raids took place during 1915, killing 181 and injuring a further 455 people.

THE DEFENCE OF BRITAIN
The defence of Britain against aerial attack, for a combination of reasons, was slow to materialise. On 13 May 1912, the Royal Flying Corps (RFC) was formed as a branch of the Army and took over the responsibilities formerly held by the Air Battalion of the Royal Engineers, which included a balloon company. In the first instance

The actor Robert Loraine learned to fly in 1910 and in September the same year he was involved in one of the first experiments of transmitting a wireless signal, in Morse code, from air to ground over Salisbury Plain. In the photograph Loraine appears to be getting instructions on how to use the Morse key.

the responsibility for home defence had been divided between the Royal Navy and the Army and it was not until February 1916 that the latter was given full control. It would be easy to criticise the government and military authorities for not acting sooner but this was a new type of warfare and lessons had to be learned and strategies devised more or less on the hoof.

Initially there were no guns specifically designed for anti-aircraft purposes so existing weapons had to be modified and others, able to elevate their barrels sufficiently to engage enemy aircraft, had to be ordered from France. Newly trained RFC pilots had to be taught fresh skills for flying and landing aircraft at night and ways had to be devised to allow airfield personnel to bring these rather elementary flying machines down safely. It should also be remembered that at the start of the First World War electronic technology for communication and navigation was at an embryonic stage of development and it would take another war to advance such technologies to a stage where they could reasonably be relied upon. In the beginning, only a few aircraft were fitted with the most basic wireless equipment that could only communicate one way, from air to ground, by the pilot tapping out Morse code messages while trying to fly his machine.

In the autumn of 1915, after the first air attacks on London in August by German airships, the RFC deployed aircraft to a number of airfields around the capital to bolster defences. These would help supplement the existing anti-aircraft guns and searchlight batteries. Now the different agencies would have to learn to work together, and from this new defence strategies would eventually emerge. Air raids on Britain continued throughout 1916 and it took the strengthened defence system a year before it achieved its first success.

ATTACK FROM THE AIR AND CONFLICT OVER CUFFLEY

On the night of 2 September 1916, Lieutenant William Leefe Robinson, flying a B.E.2c biplane from Suttons Farm airfield in Essex, successfully brought down Schutte Lanz SL 11, the first German airship to be destroyed in aerial combat over Britain. The airship crashed in a great ball of flame near the Plough public house in Cuffley, Hertfordshire with the loss of the entire crew of 16. Several reports of the incident referred to the airship as a Zeppelin and the mistake was further exacerbated by an overenthusiastic press. One of the reasons why the Schutte Lanz burned so readily was because its internal framework was made of wood rather than the metal alloy duralumin, used in the construction of the Zeppelin.

Leefe Robinson as a Lieutenant in the Worcester Regiment before he joined the Royal Flying Corps in 1915.

SL 11 was one of a combined force of 12 Navy and four Army airships sent to attack London. It was commanded by Wilhelm Schramm, an experienced pilot who was born in England in 1855 when his father worked for the Siemens Company at Woolwich. Wilhelm was sent to Germany after the death of his father in 1900 and later joined the Army, progressing through the ranks eventually to the command of airships. In his first raid on London in September 1915, Schramm's was the only airship out of a group of four to release its bombs on the dockland areas of Greenwich, Deptford, Woolwich and Millwall. Perhaps his earlier knowledge of the region as a teenager helped him identify the targets.

According to research carried out by Ray Rimell, an acknowledged expert on Zeppelin raids, Schramm crossed the River Crouch, Essex at 10.40pm on the night of 2 September and decided to approach London from the north. He flew over Chelmsford and Colchester then turned west towards Saffron Walden and continued his journey to London, flying over the Hertfordshire towns of Royston and Hitchin. Tracing the route of SL 11 on a map, it does

The memorial at Cuffley, Hertfordshire to the memory of Captain Leefe Robinson VC, who brought down the first German airship (SL 11) over Britain on 3 September 1916. Local people are concerned for the future of the memorial as it has developed a distinct list, thought to be caused by tree roots undermining the foundations.

Schutte Lanz 'E' type rigid airship SL 14 built at Rheinau, Germany. She was the sister ship to SL 11 shot down at Cuffley. As there are no known close-up pictures of SL 11 it is hoped that this image will give the reader an idea of the airship's size.

appear to be an odd way to reach the capital, but Schramm was an experienced pilot and may have reasoned that an approach from the east would have brought him into contact with the anti-aircraft defences much sooner than an attack from the north. As Schramm crossed London Colney, in an effort to gain height before reaching London's defences he released six high-explosive and incendiary bombs that fell harmlessly in fields below. Continuing towards London, more missiles were dropped near Potters Bar, Enfield and Edmonton that killed three racehorses, damaged property and disrupted water supplies, but no human casualties were recorded. By 2.10am the airship was over Alexandra Palace, Wood Green and became illuminated by searchlight batteries allowing the anti-aircraft gunners to practise their skills. The rising flak caused Schramm to veer eastward across Tottenham. He then turned northward, releasing 24 high-explosive and three incendiary bombs on Ponders End and Enfield Highway that damaged several houses and ruptured a water main, but fortunately again there were no human casualties.

SL 11 was finally spotted by three pilots from No. 39 Home Defence Squadron who attempted to engage the airship but they were unsuccessful. Lieutenant William Leefe Robinson, who had just lost his prey, Zeppelin LZ 39, in cloud, gave up that particular chase and looked about for another opportunity. Seeing Schramm's airship illuminated by shell bursts, he headed towards it. He came up underneath and emptied the magazine from his Lewis gun as he raked SL 11 from stem to stern; the bullets appeared to have no effect. Breaking away, Robinson clipped another magazine of

Leefe Robinson in his B.E.2c aircraft after shooting down SL 11. On the left are two ground crew displaying the centre wing section inadvertently shot away by Robinson in flight.

ammunition to his gun and proceeded to rake the envelope of the airship beneath once more; still no effect. In a final attempt Robinson decided upon a new strategy, this time concentrating all his fire in one place to the rear of the airship. This time he was successful as he observed a dull pink glow coming from inside the envelope. In Robinson's words, "In a few seconds the whole rear part was blazing…I quickly got out of the way of the falling blazing Zeppelin and being very excited fired off a few red Very lights and dropped a parachute flare. Having very little oil and petrol left, I returned to Sutton's Farm landing at 2.45am. On landing I found that I had shot away the machine gun wire guard, the rear part of the centre section, and had pierced the rear main spar several times."

Rolls of SL 11's reinforcing wire being removed from the crash site. In the background, to the left, can be seen old St Andrew's church.

Sightseers on the platform of Cuffley Station, waiting for a return train to London.

Leefe Robinson's VC on display at Christie's Auction House, London in 1988 prior to the start of bidding. In a short time bidding reached £99,000.

Crowds of Londoners and spectators across the Home Counties witnessed the demise of SL 11. Although the time was after two in the morning, people had been awakened by the drone of airship engines, the sound of bombs exploding and the repeated noise from the gun batteries. Upon going outside their homes they were not disappointed by what they saw. Reports suggest that when SL 11 exploded in flames, the light was so bright it could be seen over a radius covering 60 miles, from Reigate in the south to Cambridge in the north. Newspapers the following day made much of the story and Robinson became a national hero literally overnight as his action had given flagging public confidence a much-needed boost. For the first time the public had witnessed that Britain had an answer to those leviathan invaders and their crews whom the popular press had dubbed "baby killers". For his gallantry Robinson was awarded the Victoria Cross. The announcement of the decoration came within two days of his success, one of the fastest recommendations in the history of the medal.

Station Road, Cuffley 3 September 1916 completely jammed with traffic as people came to view the wreckage of SL 11. Cuffley railway bridge can be seen in the background.

Souvenir hunters searching the SL 11 crash site for mementos on the day that became known as "Zepp Sunday".

Robinson's successful downing of SL 11 was due to the new incendiary ammunition that had recently been introduced into the RFC squadrons. The bullets named after their inventors or manufacturers were known as Buckingham, Brock, Pomeroy and "Sparklets", the latter after the popular soda siphon bulb. Normally the ammunition would be loaded into the gun's magazine as a mixture of rounds with normal 0.303-inch bullets. The idea being that the 0.303 round would pierce the airship's highly volatile hydrogen bags, allowing the gas to leak and mix with the air inside the envelope where it could be ignited by the incendiary bullets.

The wreckage of SL 11 being examined by military personnel.

THE POTTERS BAR ZEPPELIN

Almost a month after the downing of the Cuffley airship another victory was claimed in the skies over Hertfordshire with the bringing down of one of Germany's super Zeppelins, L 31, at Potters Bar. This was a new breed of airship of massive size, with a length of just under 200 metres and a width of 24 metres. Although the top speed of these monsters was a little over 60 miles per hour, they had an upper ceiling approaching 20,000 feet (6,096 metres), putting them easily beyond the range of the defending RFC squadrons and also the anti-aircraft batteries. However, these high climbers suffered severe disadvantages of extremely cold temperatures at altitudes that saw instruments and engines freeze. The rarefied air at these heights caused crew members to suffer airsickness, fainting from lack of oxygen was often experienced and frostbite was not uncommon. To navigate and to identify targets, particularly if above cloud, the airship would have to descend, making it vulnerable to attack from both aircraft and guns.

German Navy Zeppelin L 31, that was brought down over Potters Bar, Hertfordshire by Lieutenant W.J. Tempest on the night of 2/3 October 1916.

On the night of 2 October 1916, Zeppelin L 31 commanded by the German airship ace Heinrich Mathy was approaching London from the northeast. After making landfall near Lowestoft, Suffolk at around 8pm he proceeded down country and at 9.45pm he was picked up by the Kelvedon Hatch searchlight. Mathy managed to avoid their attention by turning northwest before continuing his approach to London. He skirted around the towns of Hertford and

Ware then, north of Waltham Abbey, he came under an intense barrage from two separate gun batteries. This forced Mathy to release his complete bomb load over Cheshunt in an effort to gain height away from his hostile reception. The bombs damaged over 300 houses and destroyed six and a half acres of the Lea Valley horticultural industry's glasshouses.

Kapitan Heinrich Mathy and his wife, taken in 1915. Mathy and the entire crew of L 31 perished when Lieutenant W.J. Tempest brought down the Zeppelin in flames over Potters Bar, on the night of 2/3 October 1916.

Also on the night of 2 October, Lieutenant Wulstan Tempest was airborne in a B.E.2c, patrolling a sector across the River Thames, backwards and forwards, from his home airfield at Sutton's Farm, Essex to another airfield at Joyce Green, near Dartford, Kent. Tempest's personal account shows that he was not too happy with his assignment as he remarked, "the futility of being restricted to a ceiling of 8,000 feet, when it was common knowledge among those with experience of Zeppelin chasing that these ships rarely flew at an altitude of less than 12,000 feet, and often reached a height of 15,000 feet. How could one expect to 'pot' them with such a handicap?" Tempest decided to ignore his orders and changed course for central London, circling and climbing to gain height over the capital. Glancing at his watch he saw that the time was approaching midnight. Then, all of a sudden, searchlight beams began to penetrate the night sky and illuminate the unmistakable shape of a Zeppelin to the north.

Tempest estimated the airship to be 15 miles away at a height of between 15,000 and 16,000 feet, on a heading towards London and diving at a steady rate as it flew. Turning his aircraft in the direction

Three members of B Flight from Suttons Farm, Essex all of whom received decorations for bringing down German airships. From left to right, Flight Commander W.L. Robinson, VC, Lieutenant W.J. Tempest, DSO, and Lieutenant F. Sowrey, DSO.

of the Zeppelin, Tempest flew towards her at about 90 miles per hour just as the anti-aircraft batteries opened up below. Ignoring the danger, he pursued his quarry. At five miles from the airship Tempest was now higher than his prey and estimated the ship's height to be "considerably below 10,000 feet". As Tempest came closer he was caught in the middle of the anti-aircraft barrage with shells bursting all around him. Continuing his pursuit Tempest saw the Zeppelin release all her bombs; this would have been when the airship was over Cheshunt, as mentioned earlier. The airship's manoeuvre caused Tempest to believe it had been done specifically to gain height in an effort to shake him off, rather than to avoid the hostile gunfire from below.

Just as Tempest was about to engage the Zeppelin, the B.E.2c's petrol pump failed and he was forced to use the hand-operated pump. He was now flying very close to the Zeppelin and still slightly higher. Realising that his quarry could climb out of reach at any moment, Tempest put his aircraft into a dive and came up underneath the airship, strafing her with his Lewis gun as he flew beneath her. Although he was using Buckingham and Pomeroy incendiary ammunition laced with 0.303-inch ordinary bullets, his strafing run achieved nothing. Tempest made a second run beneath the airship from the rear, this time putting in another burst from the Lewis gun; still no effect. Banking away from the airship and avoiding her hostile fire Tempest came round and placed his aircraft under the ship's tail section out of the way of her machine guns. While there Tempest let off another burst and this time he was successful as he saw a red glow coming from inside the Zeppelin's envelope, which he described as looking "like an immense Chinese lantern". How Tempest managed to fly and manoeuvre his aircraft while hand-operating the petrol pump and aiming and firing his Lewis gun we shall never know.

As the fire took hold, the Zeppelin, in her death throes, shot upwards around 200 feet, probably due to expanding hydrogen in her gas bags, hung in the air for a few seconds and then began to fall. Tempest must have been mesmerised by the sight, as his description of the scene is one of awe. "Flames burst from her glowing envelope and licked her bows. Brighter they grew, ruby orange, yellow, paler. And then she seemed to be coming straight for me." Realising he was in mortal danger of being consumed by the falling leviathan, he frantically put his aircraft into a nose dive to escape and was lucky not to be caught by the burning wreckage which he described as "tearing down on me". Tempest, thinking quickly, put his aircraft into a spin and managed to "corkscrew" his machine out of the way as the blazing body of the Zeppelin roared past him. Still in awe of what he was witnessing, his eyes followed the flaming hulk all the way to the ground where on impact a cloud of sparks shot skyward. In his excitement Tempest fired off, "dozens of green Very lights in the exuberance of [his] feelings".

A man up the tree attaching a rope to some of L 31's bracing girders. Most of the Zeppelin's remains were taken away by the military for examination.

Coming round from the surreal experience, Tempest realised he had no idea where he was. He had no recollection of how long the Zeppelin engagement had lasted, neither was he sure how far he had travelled. As he wrote of the encounter, "I had lost all sense of time and direction". When analysing the experience some time later he wrote, "I am firmly convinced now that I

The Zeppelin oak, as it became known, in the driveway of No. 9 Tempest Avenue (photograph taken c.1935). To the right of the tree is No.7.

momentarily fainted in the air. When I came to, I imagined I was flying out to sea. I was positive I could see the grey waves below". To try and identify where he was, Tempest brought his aircraft down to 5,000 feet and after a while he recognised the airfield at North Weald Bassett near Epping, Essex. Coming in to land, Tempest misjudged his height and overturned his aircraft, cracking his head on the butt of his Lewis gun. He was pulled from the damaged machine by ground crew and carried shoulder high in jubilation off the landing field. His injuries amounted to "a slight cut and a bad headache which an X-ray examination afterwards showed to be a fractured skull".

The next day, Tempest made his way to Potters Bar to view the crash scene and although his experience seems somewhat ironic, by what he wrote of the occasion it would suggest that he was a very modest man. "The blackened skeleton of the vanquished monster lay across two fields, and the enterprising farmer to whom they belonged was making a charge at the gate. I paid my shilling and went in." For his gallantry, Tempest was awarded the DSO on 13 October 1916.

A NEW TYPE OF BLITZ

By mid-1917 the Zeppelin invasion of Britain which, for many reasons, is now regarded as generally ineffectual, was virtually over. Compared with the carnage on the Western Front, relatively few lives had been lost. However, the Zeppelin campaign had tied up scarce British resources, holding back over 17,000 men in defence of the Home Front who could have been deployed to supplement the Allied troops in Europe and elsewhere.

After the scaling back of Zeppelin raids, the Blitz continued with the new heavier-than-air machines, the Gotha bombers. These aeroplanes posed a more terrifying threat than their predecessors. On 25 May 1917 21 Gothas carried out their first daylight attack on Britain with a raid on Folkestone, Kent, killing 95 people and injuring 195 others. The following month, on 5 June, 22 bombers

Amusing postcards that were no doubt produced to improve the morale of British citizens who were suffering the psychological effects of the world's first Blitz.

Hark ! I hear a Zeppelin !

attacked Shoeburyness, Essex and Sheerness, Kent. On this occasion one of the raiders was brought down by anti-aircraft fire. The worst aerial attack of the War took place on 13 June, when London became the target. Fourteen (some estimates suggest 18) Gothas dropped up to 100 bombs, killing 162 and injuring 432 people. The attacks by aeroplanes rather than airships presented the RFC pilots with a new challenge. Unlike the Zeppelins, the Gothas could not be seen from a distance and were only encountered when the RFC were on top of them. Now RFC pilots would have to develop and learn new skills. Sadly, this is the continuing story of war where each new technical development, when introduced, has to be "trumped" by the opposing side.

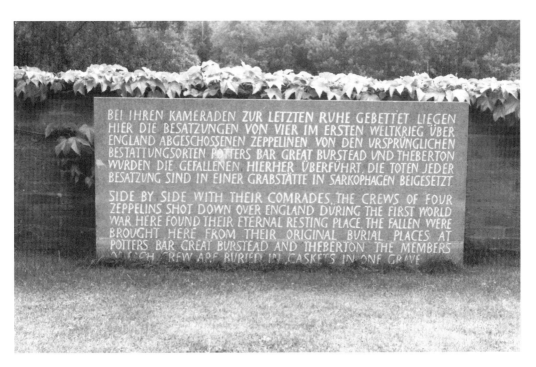

BEI IHREN KAMERADEN ZUR LETZTEN RUHE GEBETTET LIEGEN HIER DIE BESATZUNGEN VON VIER IM ERSTEN WELTKRIEG ÜBER ENGLAND ABGESCHOSSENEN ZEPPELINEN VON DEN URSPRÜNGLICHEN BESTATTUNGSORTEN POTTERS BAR GREAT BURSTEAD UND THEBERTON WURDEN DIE GEFALLENEN HIERHER ÜBERFÜHRT. DIE TOTEN JEDER BESATZUNG SIND IN EINER GRABSTÄTTE IN SARKOPHAGEN BEIGESETZT

SIDE BY SIDE WITH THEIR COMRADES THE CREWS OF FOUR ZEPPELINS SHOT DOWN OVER ENGLAND DURING THE FIRST WORLD WAR HERE FOUND THEIR ETERNAL RESTING PLACE THE FALLEN WERE BROUGHT HERE FROM THEIR ORIGINAL BURIAL PLACES AT POTTERS BAR GREAT BURSTEAD AND THEBERTON THE MEMBERS OF EACH CREW ARE BURIED IN CASKETS IN ONE GRAVE

The German war graves of aircrew at Cannock Chase, Staffordshire. In 1966 the remains of the crews of airships SL 11, L 31, L 32 and L 48 were exhumed from their resting places in various English churchyards and re-interred at Cannock Chase.

REFERENCES

Bennett, J.E. (2000) *The Story of the Potters Bar Zeppelin*, Occasional Papers No.1, Potters Bar & District Historical Society.

Cole, Christopher and Cheesman, E.F. *The Air Defence of Britain 1914–1918*, London: Putnam.

Liddle, Peter H. (1987) *The Airman's War 1914-1918*, Poole: Blandford Press.

Raleigh, W., and Jones, H.A. (1922–37) *Official History of the War: The War in the Air*, Vols. I-VI and Volume of Appendices, Oxford: Clarendon Press.

Rimell, Raymond Laurence (1984) *Zeppelin! A Battle for Air Supremacy in World War 1*, London: Conway Maritime Press Ltd.

Taylor, John W.R. (1974) *A History of Aerial Warfare*, London: Hamlyn Publishing.

Tempest, Major W.J. (2000) "How I Shot Down the L 31 Zeppelin", *The Journal of the Potters Bar & District Historical Society* No.5, Potters Bar & District Historical Society.

Note 1
During the First World War only five airships were brought down over Britain
– SL 11, Cuffley, Hertfordshire, 3 September 1916; L 32, Billericay, Essex, 24
September 1916; L 33, Little Wigborough, Essex, 24 September 1916; L 31,
Potters Bar, Hertfordshire, 2 October 1916; and L 48, Theberton, Suffolk, 17
June 1917.

Note 2
After the deaths of German airship personnel in Britain, they were usually
buried in churchyards near to where the crash took place. Later, in 1966,
their remains were exhumed and laid to rest at the German War Graves
Cemetery at Cannock Chase, Staffordshire.

Note 3
The first airship to be brought down in aerial combat during the First World
War was LZ 37. The pilot responsible was Royal Navy Air Service (RNAS)
Flight Sub-Lieutenant Reginald Alexander John Warneford. The Zeppelin was
brought down over Ghent, Belgium on 7 June 1915 when Warneford
released a number of bombs on her from above.

2. PONDERS END AND THE WORLD'S FIRST "INVISIBLE" WAR

Much has been written about the physical side of the Great War with graphic descriptions of flooded trenches, glutinous mud, unrelenting shelling, vicious barbed wire and the extreme suffering of both Allied and German troops. However, historians have paid less attention to the embryonic and emerging electronic technology that completely revolutionised the conduct of the Great War and would also dictate the pattern and strategies for wars to come. This technology began life in the Lea Valley at Ponders End, Enfield.

Professor Sir Ambrose Fleming (1849–1945) the inventor of the diode valve, the world's first thermionic device, patented in 1904. From the diode grew the multimedia electronic communications industry that surrounds us today.

THE ELECTRONIC BREAKTHROUGH

The big breakthrough in electronic technology came early in the 20th century, when, in 1904, Professor Ambrose Fleming, while working in the Lea Valley, invented the world's first thermionic device, the diode (two-electrode) valve. This was the first time that scientists had the control of a stream of electrons by electronic means (the multimedia industry of today can be traced back to this particular discovery). Although Fleming did not register his patent (No. 24850) until 1904, he had probably not realised the significance of the device, which had been produced earlier purely to understand the mechanisms that caused a blackening effect in early electric lamps. Joseph Wilson Swan, the inventor of the incandescent lamp, had called in Fleming to examine the effect and his experiments were conducted at the Edison and Swan Electric Light works at Ponders End, Enfield. Fleming's subsequent work with the Marconi Wireless Telegraph Company, then based in Chelmsford, Essex, no doubt caused him to think of improved ways of detecting wireless (radio) waves, which led him to retrieve his experimental devices from a cupboard at Ponders End. The breakthrough he achieved

The last remaining building, dated 1890, that stands on the site of the former Edison and Swan Electric Light Company Limited, Duck Lees Lane, Ponders End, Enfield.

can be called the beginning of the post-industrial revolution – the electronic technological revolution.

GUGLIELMO MARCONI ARRIVES

In February 1896, only 18 years before the world became embroiled in its first global conflict, Guglielmo Marconi, the inventor of wireless, came to England; and by August of that year, the War Office had arranged a conference to discuss the military implications of his inventions. Marconi gave a demonstration of his equipment by transmitting a signal over a distance of 20 yards between two adjoining rooms. Two days later Marconi carried out further experiments on Salisbury Plain. These were attended by the Post Office Chief Engineer, W.H. Preece and Captain H.B. Jackson, later to become Sir Henry B. Jackson, the First Sea Lord. Jackson, as an early wireless enthusiast, clearly had a good grasp of the future potential of this new medium, as he wrote of the occasion: "It may be of interest to state that the energy consumed by this apparatus to transmit signals [two miles] at Salisbury was 13 watts, that for working the masthead flashing lamp being about 260 watts."

A plaque commemorating the work of Sir Joseph Wilson Swan, Sir James Dewar and Sir Ambrose Fleming, sponsored by the Institute of Physics and campaigned for by the author for many years. The plaque, erected on the front wall of the former Ediswan building, was unveiled by the Mayor of Enfield, 10 June 2004.

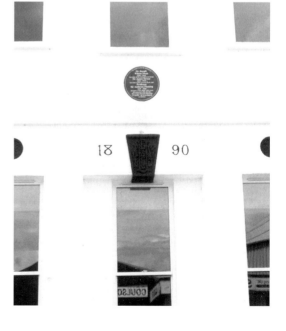

A painting of Marconi demonstrating his wireless equipment to members of the Post Office and the military on Salisbury Plain in 1896.

The Marchese Marconi, GCVO, LLD, DSc, the man who gave the world wireless (radio) communication.

Sir Henry B. Jackson (1855–1929), the First Sea Lord who was probably the first military commander to grasp the potential of wireless communication.

Over the coming months several demonstrations took place, with experiments becoming more varied and challenging. In 1899, before the military authorities at Aldershot, Marconi successfully demonstrated that wireless communication could take place between two tethered balloons spaced some distance apart, a landmark experiment before the arrival of powered flight.

During the Boer War, in 1899, five sets of wireless equipment were sent to South Africa to provide ship-to-shore communication to assist the disembarkation of troops. The exercise, however, was beset with poor reception and other problems. For some unknown reason the War Office changed the original disembarkation plan and put the equipment directly into the field, then compounded their mistake by supplying the wrong aerial masts. Fortunately, the Admiralty must have been gifted with the power of foresight as they acquired three sets of the equipment. These were installed on Royal Navy ships and, during their 1899 manoeuvres, tests were carried out to check their suitability for communication at sea. The Admiralty were obviously delighted with the results and orders were placed with the Marconi Company for a further 26 sets for Royal Navy ships and another six sets for their coastal stations. It would therefore seem fair to conclude that at least this branch of the military had recognised the value and the future potential of wireless, although there were some within the armed forces who remained sceptical of its usefulness.

WIRELESS EXPERIMENTS BY THE MILITARY

The years prior to the Great War saw many experiments by the military in wireless communication with equipment installations on land, at sea and in the air. Not surprisingly it was the last that presented the greatest technical challenge. The weight of the equipment (up to 200 pounds) could alter an aircraft's flying performance, not to mention the valuable space it could occupy in these cramped early flying machines. There was also the problem of the wireless spark transmitter presenting a potential fire hazard, as the aircraft were constructed from highly flammable materials. In addition, as might be expected, there was the requirement to generate sufficient power to run the equipment when airborne.

The introduction of the wireless caused major practical problems for the pilot too. Not only had he to fly and manoeuvre the aircraft when tapping out a message with a Morse key strapped to his knee, but he also had to observe and report movements and other events on the ground. It was probably such difficulties that caused General Grierson to remark, during airship manoeuvres in August 1912, that "the airship was of more use to me than the aeroplane, as being fitted with wireless telegraphy, I received messages in a continuous stream, and immediately after the observation was made". Although the airship as a weapon of war had it own particular drawbacks, nevertheless it could outperform the early aircraft regarding the load it could carry and the electrical power it could generate for its wireless equipment.

In August 1914, shortly after the British Expeditionary Force arrived in France, only three aircraft had been fitted with wireless equipment. At the time communication with these aircraft was only one way, from air to ground, and the medium employed was wireless telegraphy (W/T). This was Morse code and only spark transmitters were in use. The high levels of engine noise and vibration made it impossible for pilots to hear clearly the Morse signals sent by ground stations and this was why wireless communication was initially only practical one way.

SPOTTING FOR THE GUNS

By the third week of September 1914, two aircraft fitted with wireless had been assigned to artillery observation duties and it is clear from early accounts that wireless technology was changing the way battles were planned and fought. *The Short History of No. 9 (Bombing) Squadron* tells us, "The demand for the two wireless machines flown by Lewis and James became instant and Battery and Corps commanders were generous in their estimates of the value of their work". Their work was "flash spotting" (detecting the positions of enemy guns that were usually camouflaged) and also directing firepower (ranging). This helped to concentrate Allied shelling and more or less guaranteed target accuracy for the gunners.

Typically the operation worked by the artillery commander giving the pilot, before takeoff, the enemy targets he wished to destroy. They would agree upon a time when the bombardment would commence. At the designated time the observing aircraft would appear over the Allied gun battery, the trailing wireless aerial (100 or so feet of copper wire with lead weights on the end) would be wound out, the transmitter switched on and a call made to the battery wireless operator indicating all was ready. Firing would commence and the pilot then observed the fall of shot. This was communicated to the gun battery wireless operator in a pre-determined code – "left", "right", "over" and "short". Next there would be a pause while the battery commander re-sighted his guns and the fall of shot was again observed. Usually after a few such adjustments the pilot would signal "OK", meaning a direct hit. The introduction of two-seater aircraft with an observer to carry out the task of spotting and communication was a godsend for the pilot, allowing him to concentrate on flying his machine and manoeuvring his way through hostile fire without the problems of operating the Morse key.

EARLY WIRELESS LIMITATIONS

Wireless telephony, the next major breakthrough in communication technology, had some way to go in its development before it would allow good two-way contact between aircraft and ground and also between aircraft. To do this required a continuous wave transmitter that allowed speech to be sent rather than Morse. The early spark transmitters, used for Morse, were technically incompatible with the new medium. The modulation of the continuous wave with speech would require the introduction of improved types of thermionic valve that allowed engineers the capability to design wireless receivers that were more sensitive and selective (having the ability to tune between stations on different frequencies).

While unquestionably a groundbreaking discovery, Fleming's diode was capable only of the detection of wireless signals and could not amplify or become incorporated into circuitry that improved signal sensitivity and selection. These advances came later as engineers added further electrodes to the valve; the triode (three-electrode) was the next significant step forward. However, it took a war to further accelerate this technology as both sides strove to gain the military high ground. Interestingly, the British public had to wait until 1922 to reap the civil benefits of the valve with the launch of the radio station 2LO by the British Broadcasting Company (the British Broadcasting Corporation, or BBC, was not formed until 1926). Sadly it seems that war is the motivation for the advancement of many new technologies.

DESIGN AND DEVELOPMENT ENGINEERS RECRUITED

The opportunity to take airborne wireless forward came when several Marconi engineers received wartime commissions and at least three of them – Major C.E. Prince, Captain Henry Joseph Round and Captain J.M. Furnival – were heavily involved in solving the problems of aircraft speech communication. Round had considerable experience of valve development and it was probably no coincidence that he had been selected to work with his former colleagues. Most of this experimental work was carried out at Brooklands airfield, where No. 9 Squadron RFC had reformed in January 1915 under Captain H.C.T. Dowding. The work of the engineers must have been relatively successful as, when mentioning Prince, Dowding recalled that "He evolved a wireless telephone in May 1915, and I believe that the first wireless

First World War Marconi
aircraft wireless type AD 1.

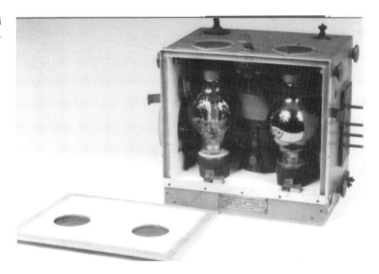

Captain Henry Joseph Round
the talented Marconi
engineer. Round was
responsible for making
considerable improvements
to thermionic valves and he
was also responsible for the
design and development of
the direction-finding
equipment that was installed
along Britain's east coast
during the First World War.

telephone message was received by me at Brooklands during that
month". However, it was not until almost the end of the war, in July
1918, that just two RFC squadrons on the Western Front were fitted
with the latest wireless telephony equipment.

The delay in equipping the RFC with the latest technology was because of major problems encountered in the design of suitable microphones that would allow clear speech to be sent above the roar and vibration of the aircraft engine. This meant designing appropriate microphone screening and making the devices capable of adjustment to cope with the differing levels of noise and vibration produced by different types of aircraft. It is probably fair to assume that Britain was ahead of Germany with this latest wireless technology. The evidence for this comes from a "Special Order of the Day", issued by the German military, offering 10,000 marks for a British aircraft compelled to land behind the German lines with its wireless telephone equipment intact. So concerned were the Allies that their new technology should not fall into enemy hands that aircraft fitted with wireless telephony were not allowed to fly over the German lines until the latter stages of the war.

A First World War portable wireless trench receiver and transmitter. These units could also be mounted on motorcycles.

STRATEGIES CHANGE

Wireless completely transformed the way the Great War was fought by both the Allies and their German opponents. At the beginning, the main method of communication on the ground was by telephone along an almost 500-mile front. Constant shelling continually cut the telephone cables and communication relied on runners, carrier pigeons and dispatch riders. The early introduction of portable crystal receiving sets (not requiring a battery) and portable battery-powered spark transmitters immensely improved communication between the troops in the front-line trenches and Corps headquarters situated some distance behind the lines. The Marconi Company was responsible for supplying much of this equipment to the Allies.

A wireless operator on the Western Front taking down a message received on a trench set.

A mobile wireless transmitter and receiver developed to be used on a wagon. These units were used successfully in the Middle East campaigns where mobility was essential. However, on the Western Front, the wagons with their heavy equipment and batteries often became bogged down in the glutinous mud.

KNOWLEDGE SHARING

It might seem to the casual observer that Britain led Germany in wireless technology. After all, it was the British military and the Post Office that had supported Marconi's early experiments. However, research has shown that before and during the war years there was a considerable amount of in-depth technical material published in periodicals like *The Marconigraph, Wireless World, Aeronautical Engineering, The Aeroplane* and *Flight*. All this information was in the public domain so it would have been easy for Germany to keep abreast of some of the new technical advances. Also, prior to January 1911, one of Europe's most formidable wireless companies, Telefunken, had been in direct competition with the Marconi Company for maritime contracts. On 14 January 1911, to overcome licensing and other contract difficulties, a joint holding company was formed out of Telefunken, Marconi and Compagnie Générale de Télégraphie Sans Fil of Brussels. The new company was called Deutsche Betriebsgesellschaft für drahtlose Telegraphie (DEBEG) of which Marconi and the Belgian company had 45 per cent interest and Telefunken the remainder. Here is clear evidence that both Britain and Germany shared knowledge of the evolving technology. It is also known that Marconi and Telefunken engineers exchanged visits as late as July 1914. Therefore, it must be assumed that the only probable technological advantage at the start of the Great War, for either side, would have been the amount of wireless equipment deployed on the battlefield. We know from the records that government placed only meagre orders with British manufacturers so wireless deliveries to the front were initially low. This would account for the use of the more traditional forms of communication at the beginning of the conflict.

CODE BREAKING – A NEW CHAPTER OF WARFARE

When hostilities began in 1914, one of the first actions of the British was to cut the German links to the transatlantic telephone cables, forcing Germany to rely on wireless as her only means of communicating with her far-flung colonies, with America and, most importantly, her shipping. It is probable that the Germans had anticipated the cutting of the transatlantic cables as the power of the wireless transmitter at Nauen, just outside Berlin, had been considerably increased by the outbreak of war. This forced reliance on wireless by the Germans and created another chapter in technological warfare, that of signal encryption and code breaking, presenting a new range of intellectual challenges for both sides. Further new counter measures were developed when it became obvious that transmitting on the same frequency as your enemy (jamming) could seriously disrupt his ability to communicate; and of course, wireless opened up the possibility of deliberately feeding your opponent disinformation. The invisible war had really begun in earnest.

It is clear that the British authorities had been unprepared for the hurried change in German communication strategy as it was not until late in 1914 that Captain (later Admiral Sir) William R. Hall, established what was to become the famous Room 40 in the Admiralty Old Building. It was there that Hall began assembling a growing number of cryptographers whose daily task was to decipher and analyse the intercepts arriving at the Admiralty from a number of different sources. It took time to bring together the right mix of people and to develop the skills needed to be able to play a meaningful role in the early days of signals intelligence. However, from these modest beginnings, it was wireless technology that became the catalyst for the establishment, through several metamorphoses, of today's famous Cheltenham establishment, Government Communications Headquarters (GCHQ), the British nerve-centre of signals intelligence (SIGINT).

WE KNOW WHERE YOU ARE!

The Marconi Company had been particularly innovative during the early part of the war and had adapted some of its peacetime maritime wireless technology to aid the war effort. In November 1914 a small number of covered trucks left the Marconi Works in

New Street, Chelmsford for France loaded with wireless direction-finding (D/F) equipment and accompanied by experienced operators. Once set up, the equipment was to prove invaluable to the Allies, as by the method of triangulation (using at least two D/F stations suitably spaced apart), any enemy wireless source could easily be pinpointed with a reasonable degree of accuracy the minute the hostile transmitter was switched on. This meant they were now vulnerable to attack.

To track the movements of the German High Seas Fleet, the Marconi Company had constructed a line of D/F stations along the east coast from Kent to Scotland. H.J. Round was mainly responsible for the D/F station design and development. The success of the D/F stations and the value of the emerging technology can be gauged by considering the strategy employed by the Admiralty during one of Britain's most famous sea battles.

While the stations were monitoring German naval wireless traffic it was noted that the principal wireless ship, the "Bayern", and those answering her had moved 1.5 degrees, a particularly precise measurement considering this technology was still in its infancy and the electronic components to improve sensitivity and accuracy had yet to be developed. Remarkably, this small movement suggested that the German fleet had moved from its base at Wilhelmshaven, had taken up a position in the Jade River and was about to put to sea. It is likely that the D/F station at Hunstanton, on the Norfolk cliff top, was one of those involved with triangulating the bearing. What is also remarkable is that the distance between Hunstanton and the German fleet was almost 300 miles.

Admiral Sir John Jellicoe, commander of the Grand Fleet. Jellicoe was able to put to sea a day early to engage the German Battle Fleet at the Battle of Jutland as the east coast D/F stations had been monitoring German naval wireless traffic and had noted that some of their ships had moved.

The information of the movement was communicated, via landline, to the Admiralty's Room 40 and the Grand Fleet, under the command of Admiral Sir John Jellicoe, was ordered to sea a day early so that advantage might be gained over the German Battle Fleet by forcing an early engagement. The following day, 31 May 1916, the battle of Jutland commenced. This is just another example of how wireless changed the way war was fought.

The east coast D/F stations, almost by luck, could detect the position of the deadly "U" Boats when they surfaced to use their wireless and they could also follow the course of Zeppelins as they came across the North Sea to carry out bombing raids on targets in Britain. Zeppelins had the advantage of being able to fly high, the later ones being able to get above 20,000 feet, which could keep them out of range of attacking aircraft and guns. However, on many occasions the height advantage turned into a serious disadvantage for the German aircrews, as instruments and equipment would freeze, rendering them useless. On cloudy nights it was impossible to navigate a course by sighting familiar landmarks. When this happened the airship would have to call base for a wireless bearing to discover its location. A Zeppelin wishing to find its position would usually call the German control centre at Cuxhaven (in Morse code) giving its particular call sign, normally a single letter, and request permission to obtain a bearing. Once granted, the Zeppelin would transmit the letter "V" which the wireless operator would repeat for about 30 seconds. The Zeppelin's signal would be picked up by at least three fixed German D/F stations and the respective bearing between each of these and the airship would be taken. In turn these D/F stations would communicate their results to the control centre by wireless where, by triangulation,

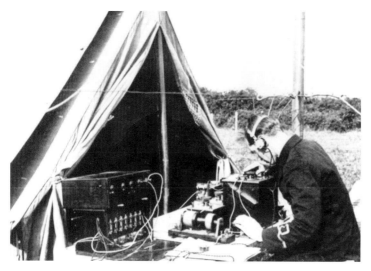

A naval wireless operator adjusting the Marconi Bellini-Tosi direction finding equipment at one of the east coast stations. This equipment could pinpoint enemy wireless sources and monitor the progress of ships, submarines and incoming Zeppelins.

The adjustable coil unit that was part of the Marconi Bellini-Tosi direction-finding (D/F) equipment.

the position of the Zeppelin would be plotted on a large-scale map. As the D/F stations had communicated their bearings to the control centre by wireless it was possible for the Zeppelin to receive this information and the navigator could plot his own position. However, it was usual for the control centre to enquire if the Zeppelin had received the information and if not the message would be repeated on higher power.

The enemy wireless traffic was gratefully received by the Marconi east coast D/F stations and the Zeppelin's course monitored as it crossed the North Sea. This information was communicated to Room 40 where the progress of the invader and any others on the raid was plotted on a chart. As the different bearings were received, the plots were moved across the chart and this not only allowed Room 40 to calculate the Zeppelin's position but also its airspeed. It was known that once over Britain the Zeppelins would have to descend to bombing height and this would render them vulnerable to attack by British aircraft as well as artillery. Room 40 collated the information passed from the Marconi D/F stations and it was then a simple task to alert the appropriate fighter stations and gun emplacements that were close to the incoming Zeppelin's path. Aircraft would be scrambled and were ready and waiting as the enemy approached. Observers on the ground would be on heightened alert listening for the first characteristic drone of a Zeppelin's engines, while the searchlight batteries and gunners anxiously waited for their opportunity to engage.

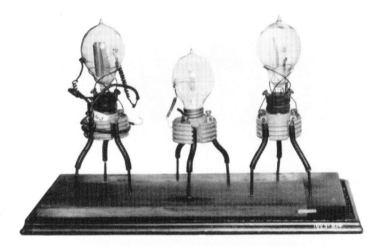

Early examples of Professor Sir Ambrose Fleming's diode valves.

Without the use of wireless the strategies described above could not have been employed and it leaves one wondering what would have been the outcome of the Great War had this new technology not come along when it did. It is doubtful if Ambrose Fleming could have foreseen, even remotely, the invisible war that his invention would bring about when he created the world's first thermionic device at a lamp works in Duck Lees Lane, Ponders End, Enfield, in London's Lea Valley.

REFERENCES

Author unknown (1936) *The Marconi Book of Wireless*, London: Marconiphone Company.

Author unknown, *Aircraft* (copy of article dated 4th June 1919, in the Marconi Archive, Bodleian Library, Oxford).

Baker, W.J. (1972) *The History of the Marconi Company*, London: Methuen.

Beesley, Patrick (1982) *Room 40, British Intelligence 1914-1918*, London: Hamish Hamilton.

Cusins, Lt. Col. A.G.T. (1921) "The Development of Army Wireless During the War", *The Journal of the IEE*, Vol. 59.

Furnival, J.M., *The Development of Wireless Technology in the RAF, 1918* (Marconi Archive, Bodleian Library, Oxford).

Jackson, Admiral of the Fleet Sir H.B. (1920) "Direction and Position Finding: discussion", *The Journal of the IEE*, Vol. 58, Part 3.

Lewis, Cecil (1936) *Sagittarius Rising*, London: Davies.

Lewis, Jim (1999) *London's Lea Valley, Britain's Best Kept Secret*, Chichester: Phillimore & Co. Ltd.

Lewis, Jim (January 1994) "The 'Weeding' of Harold Begbie", *Intelligence and National Security*, Volume 9, No. 1, London: Frank Cass.

National Archive, Kew, Air1 688/21/20/9 (1915-1937) *Short History of No.9 (Bombing) Squadron*.

Round, H.J. (1920) "Direction and Position Finding (with discussion)", *The Journal of the IEE*, Vol. 58, Part 3.

Note

The prolific Edwardian author, the late Harold Begbie, wrote a manuscript that he had intended to be published as a book entitled, *Wireless*, or possibly *Wireless in the War 1914-1918*. Sadly it was never published, because of warnings to his publisher from the military intelligence services. Begbie wished to dedicate his book to the young wireless operators, many of whom he had interviewed after the war, as he saw them as unsung boy heroes. In the second paragraph of his introduction he succinctly captures the essence of the new technology when he writes:

> Their book, which I have the honour to write, may also be called a history of the war that was never seen, that was both invisible and inaudible even to those who fought its battles, a war that was as immaterial as thought, as unsubstantial as dreams, as ethereal as personality.

3. DID THE NEW METHODS OF WEAPON MANUFACTURE IN 19TH-CENTURY BRITAIN HAVE AN IMMEDIATE EFFECT ON WARFARE?

In the earlier chapters we saw how quickly the introduction of electronic technology changed the strategy of warfare. But did the introduction of new methods of small arms manufacture have the same effect in Britain?

To answer this question it will be necessary to examine the procedures employed by the Board of Ordnance in the design and development of new weapons. It will also be necessary to discover whether British engineers possessed the essential skills, vision and inventiveness to have developed a system for the mass production of small arms manufactured with interchangeable parts, prior to the British government's purchase of machine tools from America in the mid-19th century.

However, while ease of manufacture and assembly is the Holy Grail of every plant manager, it is not necessarily correct to imagine that the introduction of a product based on interchangeable parts is the ultimate in engineering design. The reasons for this seeming paradox will be investigated within the confines of this chapter through an examination of the Ordnance system of design and procurement of new weapons.

EASE OF MANUFACTURE AND ASSEMBLY

Research to date has not uncovered any evidence to suggest that, in the first half of the 19th century, the Board of Ordnance had actively considered a change to the method by which new weapons were selected in order to ensure that designs included features improving ease of manufacture, assembly and repair. Furthermore, there appears to have been little or no thought given to a coordinated or collective approach to design which would have encouraged a more economical mode of manufacture.

Engineers had been aware for some time of the benefits of an integrated approach to product design and manufacture. The respected Ordnance engineer John Anderson, Superintendent of the Ordnance Factories at Woolwich, was well aware that weapon parts could be made more cheaply without losing their efficiency if designed with ease of manufacture in mind. In evidence to the Select Committee of 1854, Anderson demonstrated his concern for economical production methods by giving a hypothetical example of being ordered to manufacture a gun by machinery to a certain pattern, stating, "I would study to carry it out; but I should not be doing my duty if I did not say, 'By this plan you may do it much cheaper'". Moreover, it is known, from the results of research carried out that there were many complex issues surrounding the subject of economical weapon manufacture which had influenced the judgment of the Board of Ordnance. The political pressures placed upon Parliament by the private gun trade, and the long period of relative peace, following the Napoleonic Wars, were just two. As we have seen in the first book in this series, *From Gunpowder to Guns: the Story of Two Lea Valley Armouries*, it was the Crimean conflict which finally acted as the trigger for a more efficient means of military weapon manufacture by machine methods. However, research has indicated that these issues did not lead immediately to a system which deliberately set out to consider ease of manufacture at the point of product design.

Thomas Blanchard (1788–1864), an American mechanical engineer and machine tool designer.

Prior to the outbreak of hostilities with Russia, the annual output of arms from the Enfield factory was relatively small and the bulk of military weapons was being produced by manual methods by private sector contractors. Under such an arrangement, the majority of the overhead cost would have been shouldered by the private sector and not Ordnance. Therefore, there would have been little benefit for Ordnance to have pursued the preparation of new weapon designs which could be manufactured more efficiently and cheaply by machine methods. Conversely, there would have been little incentive for the private contractors to have recommended improvements in weapon design which would have no doubt increased their investment in new tools and machinery. For them, stability of product for as long as possible with minimum amount of change was all important.

Thomas Blanchard's gun-stocking machine (c.1818), currently on display in the Springfield Armoury Museum, Massachusetts. Note the machine's wooden frame.

Given these circumstances it would seem reasonable to conclude that the maintenance of the Ordnance contract system of arms procurement helped delay not only the system of machine-intensive production but also the introduction of weapon designs which were easy to manufacture. One might therefore argue, no machines, no need to modify the product. The corollary of this would seem to be to install new machines then redesign the product for ease of manufacture. But was this true in the case of the newly installed American machine tools at Enfield Lock, which had been specifically designed to manufacture a standard weapon with interchangeable parts?

NEW MACHINES AT ENFIELD

The machine tools purchased from America were installed in a new purpose-built machine room at Enfield Lock between 1855 and 1856. Through their introduction it was hoped to secure continuity of small arms supplies for the armed forces by dramatically increasing the manufacturing capacity of the factory. Because the new process was based on a system of standardised interchangeable parts, the Board of Ordnance was also expecting to see a number of economic benefits. These would range from improvements in weapon assembly times to reduced labour content per weapon, simplicity of part storage and improved stock control.

The Springfield Armoury Museum, Springfield, Massachusetts, the former site of the American Government's premier 19th-century armoury.

There would also be benefits for the military once the new manufacturing system came into service. Small arms constructed with interchangeable parts would have simplified battlefield repairs, allowing armourers with less skill and training than their predecessors to do the work. Before interchangeability, components requiring replacement at the front had to be individually made and fitted. This was costly and time consuming, not to mention problematic for the troops in need of serviceable weapons.

The introduction of the new machine tools opened up further manufacturing opportunities. There was much to be achieved by ensuring the design of future weapons took into account the limitations of machines to follow awkward shapes. Ordnance was now placed to evaluate and alter the design of those parts of the arm which had evolved over many years prior to the machine tool era. Several of these items, as Anderson had already pointed out, had complex shapes which were not essential to the effective and efficient performance of the weapon. This latter aspect will be examined later to discover if Ordnance fully appreciated the economic benefits to be gained from a programme of integrated product design linked to ease of manufacture.

An Ames Manufacturing Company gunlock bedding machine on display at the American Precision Museum, Windsor, Vermont. These machines were imported from America in the mid-19th century and installed at the Royal Small Arms Factory, Enfield.

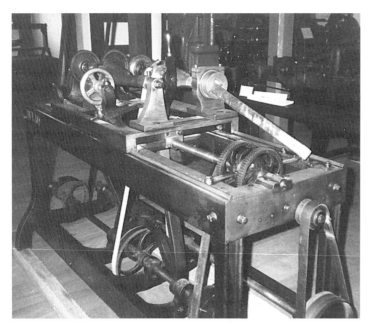

An Ames Manufacturing Company gunstock turning lathe, on display in the American Precision Museum, Windsor, Vermont. These machines along with others were installed at the Royal Small Arms Factory, Enfield and formed the basis for the UK's first mass production manufacturing system of interchangeable parts. This and others from the system can be seen at the Science Museum in London.

NEW MACHINERY, OLD-STYLE WEAPON

The new machine tools installed at Enfield had been built to accommodate the existing Pattern 1853, the design of which had evolved from earlier weapon types. In other words, the "American system" had been adapted as far as possible to fit a surviving British weapon. The Pattern 1853 had been developed as the result of an open competition in 1852 and it was not until 1854 that the British Commission to America placed orders for the new machine tools, clearly demonstrating the lack of connection between weapon design and the new manufacturing process. Looking at the weapon's historic and evolutionary development, parts of which can be traced back to 17th-century France, further confirms that the approach to manufacturing lacked coordination with design. From an examination of a range of artefacts manufactured at Enfield it can be deduced that the shape and design of certain key components of the Pattern 1853 had not been modified to favour more cost-effective production.

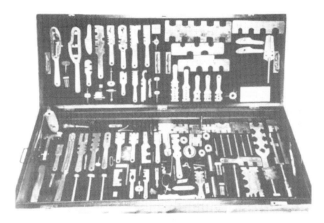

Measuring gauges for the Enfield Rifle Pattern 1853, the case also includes gauges for the lance and pike.

As the timing of the factory alterations and the installation of the new equipment at Enfield coincided with the Crimean War, it might be argued that Ordnance did not wish to experiment with weapon design changes to facilitate further manufacturing improvements. Such a decision would have seemed rational at a time when the supply of weapons to the front was absolutely crucial. However, if this was the reason, one would have expected the emergence of a strategy aimed at weapon design improvements to assist manufacture and assembly to be pursued in the more relaxed atmosphere when hostilities ceased. Later in this chapter it will be suggested that this opportunity was never grasped.

TYPICAL METHODS OF WEAPON IMPROVEMENT

During the early period, and until quite late into the 19th century, refinement of small arms design usually came about through improvements suggested by individuals. In January 1885 the

Enfield Rifle Pattern 1853, the first weapon to be made at the Royal Small Arms factory with interchangeable parts.

Inspector General of Musketry, Colonel Harrison Trent of Hythe, Kent, wrote to the Under Secretary of State for War in support of James Aston, the Civil Master Armourer, who was claiming recompense for his inventions. Between 1855 and 1882 Ashton had submitted some 15 improvements and modifications to various small arms in service, several of which had been adopted by the military. In fact, Aston had been paid £100 for three improvements he had submitted between 1855 and 1856. These consisted of a new pattern ramrod with a jag head to allow easier removal from the stock, an improved pattern lock cramp for removing the main spring and a snap-cap to fit over the nipple. All these improvements were for the Snider rifle, although the cramp could be used for the removal of similar main springs from other weapons which employed the same type of lock mechanism. Post-production modifications like the ones submitted by Aston arose from the practical experience of handling the weapon in the field and were normally designed for ease of use, not ease of manufacture. If the modification submitted could improve the weapon without both a significant on-cost and the creation of other difficulties, then its introduction would normally be given serious consideration by Ordnance or the War Office.

The clock tower of the Royal Small Arms Factory, Enfield Lock. Below this structure is a small interpretation centre showing products that were made on the site. The tower once formed part of the large machine room, specially built to accommodate the imported machine tools from America. Originally the machine room had an internal area of 180,000 square feet, which has now been turned into shops and other individual units.

Inside the large machine room, c.1990, after all the machinery had been stripped out.

It was not unusual for good ideas and designs to be taken from other manufacturers. Sometimes this came through advertisements for weapon selection by open competition or by inventors sending samples to Ordnance for evaluation. On occasion Ordnance would obtain the weapons directly for examination. In such circumstances Ordnance might negotiate a licensing or royalty agreement for incorporating these changes into their own weapons. New ideas were not limited to British inventors. In an endeavour to keep abreast of small arms development in Europe, Ordnance dispatched George Lovell, the Board of Ordnance Inspector of Small Arms and formerly the Storekeeper at the RSAF at Enfield Lock, to Germany in 1849 to examine recently introduced weapons. On his return to England he was ordered to prepare a number of muskets and rifles based on French and German patterns. Subsequently Lovell was again sent to Germany and instructed to bring back a sample of their latest breech-loaders and also a French Minié rifle. However, there is no evidence to suggest from an examination of the available reports regarding weapon change and modification that the alterations made bore any relationship to ease of manufacture or assembly. They were primarily introduced to improve aspects of battlefield handling such as firepower, range and accuracy.

Research has shown that many people were under the impression, and for that matter still are, that superiority of a particular weapon was due to the clever design and development of an individual armoury like Enfield. For example, in the House of Commons in June 1861, a leading article from *The Times* newspaper was quoted in debate. The article discussed the effectiveness of the Enfield Pattern 1853 rifle during the Crimean War by saying it "Smote the Russians like the Hand of a Destroying Angel". While the prose may seem somewhat florid and patriotic, no doubt the report helped spread the notion that the RSAF at Enfield had designed a superior weapon. This completely ignored the evolutionary process that had brought the Pattern 1853 to its eventual state of development. A further aspect, which seems to have been overlooked, is that the vast majority of Pattern 1853s supplied to the front line during the conflict were not manufactured at Enfield at all. At the time when Britain entered the war in the Crimea in March 1854, the Commission to the United States of America had only just set out on its fact-finding mission. Orders for machine tools to equip the Enfield factory were therefore not placed until later that year. The time then taken for the machines to be manufactured, shipped and installed meant that the plant did not come fully on-stream until January 1857, some ten months after hostilities had ceased.

METHODS OF WEAPON SELECTION

The second half of the 19th century in Britain saw a marked leap in the level of innovation in the evolutionary development of the small arm, resulting in a narrowing of focus towards an improved performance standard of military weaponry. This was accomplished by a method of selection through open competition between gunsmiths and inventors, rather than setting new design and performance criteria in the form of a specific research and development project. The advantage of the system of open competition was that the War Office incurred minimum development costs; the disadvantage was that little attention was paid to ease of manufacture and assembly. As has already been pointed out, the introduction of the "American system" at Enfield in the mid-1850s with sequenced machinery producing arms with interchangeable parts had little effect in moving Ordnance towards a policy of integrating weapon design with ease of manufacture. To discover why the opportunity to produce weapons more simply and economically had seemingly been ignored, it will be necessary to examine in some detail the reports of the Ordnance Select Committee on Small Arms which took place as the second half of the century got under way. In so doing, we will gain a better understanding of the criteria used by Ordnance when selecting the next generation of weapons.

Lord Raglan (1788–1855), the commander of the British troops at the Crimea. Raglan and his staff were singled out by the press for failings at the front, although there were several reasons why the British troops lacked arms and basic equipment. During his long military career, Raglan had sustained wounds in previous battles, losing a right arm at Waterloo.

At the time of the American Civil War there was considerable controversy among high-ranking British officers and government officials over the effectiveness of the breech-loading rifle in use with the Federal Troops. On 13 June 1864 the British Secretary of State for War, Lord de Grey, set up a committee to investigate the usefulness of equipping the infantry with breech-loading arms. Grey himself had considerable reservations about the breech-loader as he was of the opinion that, "troops thus armed might fire away their ammunition too rapidly, and thus increase the difficulty of supplying them with ammunition during action, and render necessary the employment of a larger amount of transport than would otherwise be required".

The Committee met for the first time on Monday 27 June 1864, under the Presidency

The American Civil War,
Battle of Pocotaligo
(22 October 1862).

A picture depicting the Battle of Olustee (20
February 1864) during the American Civil War.

of Major General Russell C.B., to consider the evidence of a number
of army officers and experts. Lieutenant Colonel Gallwey R.E. and
Captain Alderson R.A. attended and informed the Committee that
during their recent visit to America they had discovered different
opinions among the military authorities as to the value of the
breech-loader. Unfortunately these officers were not able to give a
personal account of the breech-loading rifles in action as they
explained: "the United States Secretary for War refused us
permission to accompany the army on active service". Gallwey and
Alderson said that several General and Staff Officers whom they
had interviewed "seemed to hold the opinion that breech-loading
arms, in the hands of selected bodies of troops, would be
productive of good results". A Brigadier General Seymour, a very
experienced soldier by all accounts, who had acknowledged the
usefulness of the Spencer breech-loader at the battle of Olustee,
was "averse to breech-loaders as a general weapon for infantry. He
advocates the arming of flank companies or other picked bodies
with special arms; but for the main body of infantry he would prefer
a simple smooth-bore musket". The reasons for this preference were
thought to be due to "the general nature of the country, which
being densely wooded, only admits of actions being fought at close
quarters". On the other hand, Brigadier General Terry reported that,
when he was in command at Pocotaligo, his troops were suffering
considerably from enemy fire. He therefore ordered a Colonel
commanding a regiment whose flank companies were armed with
Sharp's breech-loaders to "push forward those companies into the
best cover they could find, and open fire on the enemy". It was said
that "the men knowing that this was done to test the value of their
arms, answered with a cheer, and advanced in skirmishing order,
covering themselves as best they could. In a short time the enemy's
fire was subdued".

The second meeting of the Committee took place on Thursday 30
June 1864, when Brevet Colonel Dixon R.A., Superintendent of the

Royal Small Arms Factory, Enfield, was examined. It was reported that Dixon "considers breech-loading practicably objectionable; the prime cardinal difficulty, however, being connected with the ammunition". His main objection concerned the safe storage of certain types of breech-loading ammunition which had its own "means of combustion".

A picture of the ruins of the Harpers Ferry Armoury, destroyed during the American Civil War (1861–65).

A Major Young R.A. was examined by the Committee and reported that during his foreign tour of 1861 he had been present at the autumn manoeuvres of the Prussian troops on the Rhine when the breech-loading needle gun was used. There he had been told by Austrian officers "that the arm had been discarded from their service; and the Prussians themselves would also discard it were they not so entirely committed to its use". He also voiced similar objections to those of the Secretary of State for War when he explained "breech-loaders are not adapted for general service, but only for trained men and for special occasions; and that they are a temptation to young soldiers to fire away all their ammunition".

James Burton, the former Master Armourer at Harpers Ferry who had been brought from America to oversee the installation of the new gun-making machinery at Enfield, told the Committee that breech-loaders "are the favourite weapons of the Federal cavalry; and that the general impression in the United States is that the system will be universally adopted". This, incidentally, was also Burton's personal opinion.

The Committee appears to have been extremely thorough in its investigation, even going as far as to read extracts from a report some 15 years earlier (dated 19 October 1849) by the late Inspector of Small Arms, George Lovell. Here it was reported that Lovell had received assurances from the military authorities of the effectiveness of the Prussian breech-loading needle gun when used during the war with Denmark. Lovell had reported in his evidence that the "advantages claimed for it [the needle gun] being that it has little or no recoil, can be fired 12 times a minute, and can be fired and loaded by a soldier even when lying down or presenting his bayonet to the enemy".

Major General Hamilton C.B., late Military Attaché to the British Embassy in Berlin and at the time Vice-President of the Council of Military Education, reported that he had received "most satisfactory accounts of the needle gun… the arm has been much improved there during its 16 years since introduction, and is now the only rifle used by the Prussian infantry". It is also interesting to note that Hamilton went on to suggest that he had "never heard of any accident caused by the ammunition containing its own ignition, or of any escape of powder from the gun", which had been a major fear expressed in evidence by Colonel Dixon. Hamilton also stated that he had "never heard of any difficulty in keeping up supplies in the field". This was the basis of an earlier objection to the adoption of the breech-loader by the Secretary of State for War, Lord de Grey.

After completing four meetings between 27 June and 11 July 1864, and having listened carefully to the evidence of the various experts and military officers, the Committee decided "to report their opinion in favour of arming the Infantry wholly with breech-loading arms". Although the Committee, which comprised five Colonels under the presidency of a Major General, took the collective decision to recommend that breech-loaders should be issued to the infantry, it can be seen from the range of evidence given, that opinions were divided as to the usefulness of this weapon. While this particular debate highlights the necessity for training military personnel in the use of any new weapon and identifies potential logistical supply problems for the army, it also demonstrates quite graphically the lack of any sort of planned weapons development programme. It would therefore appear that the Committee of 1853 under John Anderson, Superintendent of the Ordnance Factories at Woolwich, who called the method of procuring small arms "heterogeneous in its character", might have used the same terminology had they been asked to investigate the then current method of designing and developing small arms for the British Army.

AN OPPORTUNITY TO CHANGE

The Ordnance contract system of arms procurement, which had operated throughout the first half of the century, had effectively denied Enfield the ability to produce weapons on a large scale. This had been achieved through political pressure exerted by the private sector on Parliament. It can also be seen from Lovell's evidence to the Select Committee of 1849 that he was opposed (at least on the surface) to the expansion of Enfield's manufacturing capabilities. These measures had allowed the factory to concentrate on a policy of keeping a "check" upon the private gun trade in both Birmingham and London. However, with Ordnance in firm control of military small arms manufacture as the second half of the century progressed, Enfield's annual output increased dramatically. Between 1858 and 1864 the factory produced in excess of 505,000 guns and pistols. Having the potential to produce such large volumes, it might seem curious that savings were not apparently being considered by making simple design changes to the weapon, particularly those which Anderson had identified earlier. With the acceptance of the breech-loader as the new weapon for the military, there was a clear opportunity to maximise the efficiency of the recently installed plant at Enfield. This could have been partly achieved by specifying a simple manufacturing and assembly clause in the open competition document, which invited tenders for the modification of the Pattern 1853 to a breech-loader. Of course there is the possibility that the War Office, having taken responsibility for arms procurement, was intent on containing the conversion cost of the Enfield rifle in the short term by stipulating in the tender notice that the alteration was "not to exceed £1 per arm".

As discussed above, from a rudimentary examination of the lock mechanism of the Pattern 1853 Enfield rifle, the shape and design of this component had changed little from its origins in 17th-century France. Carrying out the modification to a breech-loader on the Snider principle would mean that the lock design would continue into the second half of the 19th century. Therefore, there can be little doubt that successive Master Generals of Ordnance and those in authority at the War Office had not considered ease of manufacture and assembly. Consequently, it is probably fair to speculate that, as most of these men came from military and political backgrounds, their interests lay mainly in a weapon's range, accuracy and fire-power, rather than the niceties of manufacturing efficiencies. For example, Viscount Henry Hardinge in 1852 had succeeded Henry William Paget Marquis of Anglesey as Master General of the Ordnance. Both men had served with Wellington in the Peninsular Wars and both had interwoven their military careers with various political appointments. Wellington, in his long and distinguished military and political career, had himself been Master General from 1819 to 1827 and Prime Minister from 1828 to 1830.

From 1683, the office of Master General had been filled by a senior member of the military holding a Cabinet seat. This practice continued until 1828. O.F.G. Hogg has said of the situation, "The office [of MGO] therefore, came to be regarded as a prize for the most distinguished soldier of his time". It would therefore seem fair to conclude that these particular occupations were hardly the best

A painting of Arthur Wellesley (1769–1852), the Duke of Wellington, on his favourite horse, Copenhagen.

Henry William Paget (1768–1854), the Marquis of Anglesey, who lost a leg at the Battle of Waterloo. Paget was Master General of Ordnance in the period before Viscount Henry Hardinge was appointed to the post.

qualifications for appreciating and understanding the intricacies of production engineering and the cost benefits to be gained from a weapon development programme which considered ease of manufacture and assembly.

A DIFFERENT DESIGN AND DEVELOPMENT PHILOSOPHY

In contrast to British Ordnance, the American national armouries demonstrated a greater awareness of the need to constantly review and to develop methods of efficient arms production. Merritt Roe Smith, when discussing interchangeability, pays tribute to John H. Hall who "stood foremost among those who combined inventiveness with entrepreneurial skill in blending men, machinery, and precision measurement methods into a workable system of production". Although Roe Smith has recognised that Hall failed to "achieve significant economies of scale" when he produced the first "fully interchangeable weapons in the United States", he does however see him as a "pivotal figure in the annals of American industry". An illuminating point concerning Hall's expertise came from a contemporary, Eli Whitney Blake, the nephew of Eli Whitney. Meant as a criticism, he stated that Hall "had purposely designed his rifle for interchangeable production", suggesting that "whenever insurmountable technical difficulties arose, the inventor eliminated them by changing his model accordingly". Without apparently knowing it, Blake had put his finger precisely on the point, that of altering the design of a product to accommodate the needs or inadequacies of a production system.

Roe Smith has stated that there were 11 changes made by Hall to his rifle between 1823 and 1841 which were generally not "aimed at circumventing technical production problems". This might seem somewhat ironic as Roe Smith implies that the changes, rather than simplifying machine operations, "demanded even greater machining capacity". It is however conceivable that some of the early changes made by Hall were to accommodate variations from the pattern that occurred at the time when he was making certain parts by hand for the first contract guns, prior to his machinery being completed. These alterations would probably have been necessary to even out spreads created by hand finishing, thereby setting a standard for the machines. This may have been the root of a number of contract difficulties, as it is known that not all the 19,680 weapons made under Hall at Harpers Ferry were completely interchangeable. Roe Smith has pointed out that the "operating parts of the Hall rifle were more numerous and complex in design than those of the common military musket". This, he suggests, eventually provoked the War Department to cease production of Hall's weapon at Harpers Ferry in 1844.

The evidence produced by Roe Smith would seem to confirm that Hall played a "pivotal" role not only in the development of interchangeable part manufacture but also in the acceptance of the notion that product design could be changed to accommodate the then-current production technology. This latter point must be completely understood by any designer wishing to have his product made in a standardised way by mass production machinery. It is a fundamental principal that, if the technology of mass production is to work efficiently, product designers must have some knowledge of the mechanical capabilities of the machines on which their designs will be made. There is usually a strong requirement for good levels of understanding and cooperation between production engineers and designers at an early stage in the product development cycle. These concepts are certainly understood in engineering circles in the 21st century, although it would appear they had not been universally grasped in the 19th. Furthermore, those in powerful administrative positions within British Ordnance were either ignorant of the concept of designing a weapon for ease of manufacture or were ignoring it.

James H Burton (1823–94), former Master Armourer at the Harpers Ferry Armoury. In June 1855 Burton came to Enfield on a five-year contract to oversee the installation of the American machine tools.

The remaining Fire Engine House, later known as John Brown's Fort, after restoration, at Harpers Ferry Armoury.

Unlike his British Ordnance counterparts, Hall was uniquely positioned to take advantage of being both a weapon and a machine tool designer and of having the good fortune to be given a complete contract by the US government to develop his breech-loader. In contrast, the method of arms procurement operated by British Ordnance had divided the manufacture of a weapon among several different firms. These establishments were generally small and manufactured individual pieces of the weapon, having no responsibility for its design. Under such a system it was not possible to coordinate the skills of the product designer and the machine tool engineer. The luxury which Hall enjoyed simply did not exist in Britain. However, while it would appear that Hall had, either consciously or unconsciously, raised the awareness of his contemporaries to the fact that the product could be modified to assist ease of manufacture and assembly, there does not seem to be an overwhelming amount of evidence to suggest that this notion was immediately taken up by American arms makers.

It has been suggested by Professor Tim Putnam, that "the model 1842 US army rifle unlike the Pattern 1853 Enfield, had been designed to make assembly easy". This would appear to be a somewhat curious statement to make, as the lock mechanism on this weapon is almost identical to the Pattern 1853 Enfield. However, a careful comparison of the shape of the hammer on these two weapons will reveal that the US model 1842 has a much simpler profile for a machine to follow. This would make the part more economical to produce by reducing the manufacturing time. Therefore, it could be that Professor Putnam has inadvertently confused the terminology in suggesting that the model 1842 "had been designed to make assembly easy", when the operative word should have been manufacture.

It has been stated above that the Ordnance engineer John Anderson had suggested to the Select Committee of 1854 that parts of the Pattern 1853 lock could be simplified to bring about cost-effective improvements in manufacture. Studying the evidence within the report, it becomes clear that one of the parts Anderson was referring to was the hammer or cock. During the questioning of Anderson a most important piece of information is revealed which categorically confirms that, by the middle of the century, engineers of his calibre were perfectly aware that there was considerable economic benefit to be gained from modifying the product to fit the machine. After much debate within the Committee on the subject, the question was put to Anderson: "You are to be allowed to alter the gun completely from the original pattern, to make it suit the machinery, and this is all founded upon your hopes and wishes?" Anderson replied, "Nothing has been said to me about doing that; that has only been spoken about in this Committee-room. I stand by what I said on that matter". This implies that engineers, although aware of the advantages of designing product for ease of manufacture, had not been invited to do so by Ordnance. What is perhaps more significant about this piece of evidence is that the debate had taken place before Anderson went to America with his two colleagues to investigate the use of machine tools in arms manufacture, showing that engineers in Britain were already aware of the economic benefits which accompanied an integrated design and manufacturing approach.

DESIGN THROUGH COMPETITION

In August 1864, following the recommendations of the Committee on Breech-Loading Arms, the War Office issued an advertisement inviting gun-makers and inventors to submit plans to convert the Enfield Pattern 1853 from a muzzle to a breech-loader, calling for two main criteria to be met. The first was that the cost was "not to exceed £1 per arm" and the second was that "the shooting of the converted arm not be inferior to the Enfield rifle" (i.e. the unmodified muzzle-loader). On completion of the modifications, the converted weapons were to be assessed for accuracy, penetration, initial velocity, recoil, rapidity of fire, liability to failure, simplicity of management, fouling and exposure to weather. Interestingly, the Committee had made no references which might have suggested that ease of manufacture or assembly were to be considered.

The advertisement attracted 50 different applicants for the conversion work. After careful examination of the submissions, the applicants were eventually whittled down to the following eight systems, these being "the most promising for the object in view:

    1. Storm's
    2. Shepard's (b)
    3. Westley Richards'
    4. Wilson's
    5. Green's
    6. Snider's
    7. Joslyn's
    8. Shepard's (a)"

The first five of the above systems used the standard Enfield rifle cap and nipple method of igniting the charge, while the latter three had been adapted for cartridges carrying their own ignition.

To make the trial absolutely fair, the Superintendent of the RSAF selected 48 rifles from stock and had them tested for "soundness and accuracy at 500 yards' range", before they were issued (six each) to the chosen competitors for conversion. Preceding the trial, all converted rifles were subjected to the regulated proof to ensure the safety of the breech arrangement. Four rifles were selected from each individual six and assigned to experiments for range, accuracy, penetration, initial velocity and recoil. The remaining two rifles were reserved for further experiments concerning rapidity of fire, liability to failure, simplicity of management, fouling and exposure to weather. Over the coming months extensive trials were carried out and it was reported that more than 5,500 rounds were fired with only one misfire. This allowed the Committee to conclude that the converted weapons "are therefore much superior in this respect [misfiring] to the muzzle-loading Enfield". This gave the Committee members the confidence to state that "the Committee feel justified in recommending that, for the armament of the infantry, the conversion of the Enfield rifle to a breech-loader on Mr. Snider's system may now be proceeded with to any extent which the Secretary of State may deem advisable".

The final report by the Ordnance Select Committee on 21 June 1866 had resulted from an exclusive trial of the Snider-converted breech-loader against the Enfield muzzle-loader. Here the opportunity had been taken to test the latest-pattern cartridge proposed by Colonel Boxer, Superintendent of the Royal Laboratories at Woolwich.

For the final experiment, which was to prove the most severe, the Committee arranged for two of the converted rifles to be fired ten times each, then plunged into "brackish water, wholly immersing them, and allowing the barrels to become filled with water, one with a cartridge case in the barrel and one without". The rifles were then removed from the water, the barrels emptied out and the weapons laid on grass exposed to the weather. This experiment was repeated over four days and on the fifth day the rifles were examined. It was then discovered that on both samples the sliding cover of the spring of the breech block pin had rusted to such an extent that it prevented the mechanism from operating easily. The breech block had to be pressed back with the foot and as a consequence the two sections of the spring cover were forced together and the spring did not have the power to open them. In spite of this, it was reported that the rifles were still serviceable "and could be loaded with comparative ease". It was further reported that the accuracy of the rifles was affected during the firing of the first 25 rounds due to rust having formed within the barrels. However, after this short period of use the report notes that the rifles were "restored by firing to their original condition, the accuracy of the last six targets being equal to that with clean rifles". It will have been noted from the reports of the exceedingly harsh testing that the overwhelming emphasis of the trial was to observe how well the weapon performed under extremes of battlefield conditions, not how easily it could be manufactured.

Further rigorous testing followed. A rifle was selected and laid on the ground with its breech closed, whereupon sand and dirt was thrown over the mechanism. After the debris had been shaken off and removed by hand, the rifle was reported to be "at once perfectly serviceable". The experiment was repeated, this time with the breech open when it was reported "There was some difficulty in clearing the breech entirely by the hand alone, but by means of a small piece of stick picked off the ground the dirt was cleared out and the rifle was fired". After subjecting the rifle to further tests and carrying out a number of severe experiments with the "Boxer" ammunition which involved placing 20 cartridges prior to firing in a barrel of wet sawdust for periods of between 118 and 192 hours, the Committee came to the conclusion that there was:

> a considerable increase of accuracy by this system of conversion at all ranges; yet, in the opinion of the Committee, the precision at ranges beyond 700 yards is not such as will meet all the requirements of the service in the field, looking to the number of skilled marksmen in the ranks of the Army; and therefore the recommendation… that the Superintendent, Royal Laboratory, and Superintendent, Small-arms Factories, should investigate the subject of small-bore breech-loader, of 0.45 or 0.50 calibre, adapted for ammunition carrying its own ignition, should still be carried out.

The Committee in the final paragraph of their report were of the opinion that the trials of the Snider breech-loading rifle proved so satisfactory that it had:

> at length enabled them to recommend to the Secretary of State for War, the immediate armament of the British Army (if so desired), [with] a breech-loading weapon and an ammunition which in point of simplicity and general efficiency, they confidently believe will be found superior to any other with which any foreign army is provided.

Apart from the converted Snider breech-loader being the first weapon of its type to be manufactured in quantity at Enfield, it was

Carbine Cavalry Snider Mk III, 0.577 inch c.1876. It was Snider who won the competition to convert the Enfield Pattern 1853 from a muzzle-loader to a breech-loader.

the first weapon in Britain to be produced with a steel barrel in place of the traditional iron component. Although the Committee recommended that the Snider breech-loader go into service with the British Army, they had already voiced certain reservations over the weapon's "precision at ranges above 700 yards" and went on to suggest that the Superintendent at Enfield investigate the merits of a "small-bore breech-loader, of 0.45 or 0.50 calibre". This is clear evidence that, while the Committee recognised the battlefield merits of the Snider, by recommending this weapon they were accepting a compromise solution. Under the system of selection by open competition, it would be difficult, if not impossible, to arrive at anything better. It will be immediately recognised that the Committee's suggestion that Enfield should investigate the possibility of designing a weapon with a smaller calibre would, if successful, release another arm requiring a different type of ammunition creating serious problems for the Army. The issue of weapons of at least three different calibres to British soldiers had had serious consequences for the troops on the front line during the Crimean conflict.

By studying other reports issued by the Ordnance Select Committee there appears to be no evidence to suggest that the War Office had ever considered laying down a detailed specification for a new weapon, by creating a development programme from scratch. Apart from the obvious benefits of ease of manufacture which would have resulted, the problems of having different calibres of ammunition could also have been avoided by careful design. However, contained within the trials of the different breech-loading systems there is a considerable amount of information relating to experiments for accuracy, rapidity of fire, initial velocity, fouling and exposure to weather. It would, therefore, seem that the thinking of Ordnance was still heavily biased towards battlefield needs and had yet to appreciate the savings to be made in production time, labour costs, material wastage and final product cost by integrating or linking the weapon design to the manufacturing process.

As mentioned above, the Committee, in its deliberations, had referred to the report written by George Lovell some 15 years earlier, in 1849, on the subject of the Prussian breech-loading needle gun. This is perhaps an indication of the state of the technical progress within Ordnance. Surely it cannot be argued that the method of weapon development by a process of evolutionary change, as had been adopted by the War Office (which by 1856 had taken over the responsibility of weapon procurement from Ordnance), would be either faster or more efficient than a properly integrated design and manufacturing programme. Therefore, it would appear, from the adopted method of new weapon selection, that the War Office were no better at appreciating the range of benefits to be gained from an integrated design and manufacturing programme than their Ordnance predecessors. The compromise results obtained through weapon selection by open competition must surely have been predictable to the military as, at best, it only partially satisfied all the performance requirements of the small arm. On occasions there were disappointing outcomes to this method of selection when, after months of fatiguing trials, there was no weapon chosen at all. This would hardly seem the most efficient and cost-effective way of equipping the armed forces with the latest in weapon technology. Clearly the government had yet to heed fully the wisdom of John Anderson when he spoke of making the weapon fit the machine. If the War Office had understood the implications of Anderson's concepts, they would have appreciated that battles could often be won on the factory floor.

A DELIBERATE DESIGN POLICY, PERHAPS?

One might speculate that Ordnance, because of the Crimean War and the pressing need to supply small arms to the front-line troops, had taken the quite deliberate decision to commit Enfield to producing the Pattern 1853 rifle without concern for ease of manufacture. In fact, they would have had little choice, as the 1854 contracts placed with the Ames Company and Robbins & Lawrence in America had clearly specified jigs, fixtures and gauges only for this particular arm. The Enfield Pattern 1853 was the latest British weapon of the day; its introduction into military service had coincided almost exactly with the American machine-tool contract. Because of this, Ordnance would have had little option but to produce the rifle on the new manufacturing system. The pressing needs of the Crimean War would not have permitted the necessary changes to the design to improve ease of manufacture, even if this aspect had been fully appreciated. If design changes had taken place, there would have been a requirement to make subsequent alterations to the manufacturing processes. It would also have been necessary to alter or replace some of the jigs and gauges, resulting in unacceptable production delays.

The author in front of the American Precision Museum, Windsor, Vermont, the former site of the Robbins & Lawrence factory. This company supplied the Royal Small Arms Factory, Enfield with essential gauges and equipment for the manufacture of the Enfield Rifle Pattern 1853.

Historically, the Pattern 1853 had evolved out of trials ordered by Lord Hardinge in 1852, when five leading gun-makers were requested to submit suitable samples of their weapons for experiment, alongside the Minié and a rifle designed by George Lovell. It is clear from this method of weapon selection (a process of elimination by competition) that ease of manufacture and assembly was not a priority – in fact it was not part of the acceptance criteria. A decade after the introduction of the Pattern 1853, it was agreed to proceed with a new generation of weapon, the Snider breech-loader. However, it should be recognised that this weapon was only a modified Pattern 1853. Ironically, the Enfield factory coming on stream with its new system of mass production after cessation of hostilities in the Crimea had helped to increase dramatically the number of Pattern 1853 rifles in circulation to over 800,000. Under the circumstances there would have been little likelihood of getting political agreement to lay down a programme for a new arm which could be manufactured more easily. Having 800,000 rifles with the potential of being converted to the next generation of arms technology at the unit cost of only one pound would no doubt have provided a powerful incentive to ignore the potential benefits of a system based on ease of manufacture. It was the success of the "American system" at Enfield which greatly increased manufacturing output, coupled with the pressure placed upon the private sector to produce arms for the Crimea, which had boosted the number of the Pattern 1853s in military possession at the end of the war. This had provided the most likely reason for delaying, or more accurately halting, progress towards a fully integrated weapon design and manufacturing programme. The weapon design policy, which was really no more than arms by selection, can therefore be viewed as having been forced upon the

THE BRITISH FORCES AND THE CRIMEAN WAR.

PATIENT HEROES.

"WELL, JACK! HERE'S GOOD NEWS FROM HOME. WE'RE TO HAVE A MEDAL."
"THAT'S VERY KIND. MAYBE ONE OF THESE DAYS WE'LL HAVE A COAT TO STICK IT ON!"

A *Punch* cartoon lampooning the poor state of military supplies at the Crimea.

authorities by a chain of circumstances over which they had little control. This situation can be seen as resulting in the military being denied their ideal small arm for battlefield performance, as the outcome of such a scheme must inevitably lead to a compromise choice.

THE FIRST GLIMMER OF UNDERSTANDING

One of the first indications that ease of weapon manufacture was about to be considered came when an invitation was posted in October 1866 for an open competition between small-arms makers and designers. The "programme of experiments", as specified within the official War Office advertisement for weapon submissions, contained a list of the nine performance headings. Here accuracy was listed first and manufacture last. The word manufacture also appeared within the concluding report of the Special Sub-Committee on Breech-Loading Arms, dated 12 February 1868, almost as an afterthought. Little can be learned from this document of precisely what the Committee had in mind with regard to manufacture.

The nine weapons under scrutiny had been passed to Colonel Dixon, the Superintendent of the RSAF, who had estimated the cost of their separate manufacture. However, a most revealing piece of information concerning how manufacturing requirements were regarded comes to light when the Committee reported that it was unable to publish details of Dixon's costs as it was "not required by the terms of the War Office Advertisement". In spite of these reservations, it would appear that Dixon's advice had been somewhat influential, as there is the suggestion that ease of manufacture was about to be taken seriously. The Committee in their assessment of the weapons were prepared to write:"the Sub-Committee decided on placing the competitive rifles in the following order of merit, with regard to their facility of manufacture in quantity and uniform quality, those which are bracketed together being considered equal:

Burton, II
Joslyn
{ Henry
  Albini and Braendlin
  Martini
Fosbery
Peabody
Remington
Burton, I".

When the Sub-Committee came, in their conclusion, to place the weapons in merit order after completing the general trial experiments, their positions had changed to the following:

Henry
Burton, II
Albini and Braendlin
Fosbery
Burton, I
Peabody
Martini
Remingto
Joslyn

Unfortunately, it is not possible to deduce from the report whether "manufacture in quantity and uniform quality" had been taken into account in the final placing as there is no reference to the word manufacture under the heading "Conclusion".

As none of the individual arms had met all the requirements laid down in the War Office advertisement, it was stated that:"the Sub-Committee do not feel justified in recommending the Secretary of State for War to overlook the want of compliance with the qualifications and award the £1,000". The Sub-Committee then went on to suggest that disqualification from the £1,000 prize should not preclude eligibility for the £600 prize for breech mechanisms. They believed that "the following rifles, having attained a satisfactory degree of excellence in other particulars, are eligible for this prize, and place them in the irrespective order of merit:

> Henry
> Burton, II
> Albini and Braendlin
> Burton, I".

The report finally ends with the conclusion that the "Sub-Committee cannot refrain from expressing their regret that no arm submitted to them should have shown sufficient merit to render its introduction into the service advisable". Although they did go on to say "the present service arm performed well during several of the trials to which it was subjected, and proved itself in many respects an efficient military weapon. In effect, 15 months had been spent, perhaps wasted, from the time of posting the advertisement to the conclusion of the report, only to confirm that the Snider breech-loader was "an efficient military weapon".

This report, which is not untypical of others dealing with weapon assessment, illustrates quite clearly the difficulties with the system of open competition. Once again it can be observed that different weapons, because of their individual characteristics, are apt to perform differently from each other in separate categories of test. Under such a system of selection it would be virtually impossible to get one type of weapon to be outstanding in every aspect of the experiment. The episode highlights a serious flaw in the weapon-selection system, which is that, by its very nature, it can not guarantee that at the end of a trial the military will have an improved specification weapon. Even if a weapon is finally chosen after this long period of assessment, there could still be serious consequences for national security. The business of constructing jigs, tools and fixtures cannot begin until the weapon is finally chosen, adding considerably to the length of the overall development programme.

A CHANGE IN THE SELECTION PROCEDURE

Throughout the remaining period of the 19th century the progress of military weapon development relied almost exclusively upon the designs of private companies and individuals. After much deliberation between the War Office Committee, arms experts and leading gun-makers, it was eventually decided to separate the evaluation of barrels from evaluation of breech mechanisms. Rifled barrels of Henry, Lancaster, Rigby, Westley-Richards, Whitworth and Enfield, judged previously as giving the best results, were selected for competition. Limits were set for length, weight, barrel calibre and type of cartridge. After extensive tests the Committee reported that they had selected a barrel from Alexander Henry of Edinburgh, Scotland and a breech mechanism designed in Switzerland by Frederich von Martini. These two components were to be incorporated into a single weapon by workmen at the RSAF, the arm becoming known as the Martini-Henry. Here it was hoped that the initiative would create "a model long-range arm of precision". However, there was still no suggestion that the method of evaluating separate components of the rifle had been adopted to take into account ease of manufacture. From the documentary evidence it is clear that the main objective was still centred on improving the weapon's battlefield performance which had been achieved by marrying together the best breech and barrel. This new method of selection would seem to confirm that the War Office Committee had finally come to recognise that the inevitable performance compromise experienced in the past, through the choice of a single weapon by competition, could at least be ameliorated by selecting the best features of more than one gun. Also, there was the advantage that the tooling-up time for the "amalgamated weapon" could be less than the previous arm. The fact that the Martini-Henry was constructed from "off the shelf" parts would have meant that patterns, jigs and gauges were already available for copying.

Experiments to evaluate separate gun components were to become the norm throughout the development of the magazine rifle, with the introduction in 1891 of the bolt-action Lee Metford Magazine Rifle Mark 1 followed in November 1895 by the now famous bolt-action Lee Enfield Rifle Mark 1. By the time the Lee Metford went into production, there was still no evidence to suggest that ease or economy of manufacture were being seriously considered. For example, the weapon was constructed from 82 separate component parts including screws and pins which took 950 different machines to produce. There were some 1,591 production processes and, with the inclusion of accessories, the figure increases by 17 per cent to 1,863. The metal components of this weapon consisted mainly of steel, with just two being made from iron, while brass was used only for the heel-plate screws and those to secure the regimental number plate. In a lecture given to the Institute of Civil Engineers in November 1892, the then Superintendent of the

Rifle Martini-Henry Mk IV
(0.45 inch) c.1887.

RSAF Enfield, John Rigby, listed the following material processes in the manufacture of the Lee Metford rifle:

steel-analysing, testing, forging, rolling, stamping, annealing, drilling, boring, tapping and screwing, milling, turning shaping, slotting, drifting, brazing, soldering, grinding, filing, polishing, hardening and tempering, bluing and browning; as to iron-forging, turning, filing, screwing and case hardening; as to brass-casting, rolling, drawing, filing, turning, punching, screw cutting and polishing; as to wood-seasoning, turning, machining, boring, filing, oiling and polishing.

Comparing the magazine Lee Metford to the earlier and simpler muzzle-loading Enfield Pattern 1853, it will be noted that the latter took approximately 680 machines and 719 different operations and processes to produce the 61 parts of this weapon. From the two sets of production figures it can be seen that the average number of machines required to produce a single part remains similar at just over 11. However, it will be noted that the average figure for processes per part has increased dramatically from 11.8 for the Pattern 1853 to 19.4 for the Lee Metford, an increase of over 39 per cent. This comparison suggests that as the complexity of the weapon increased there had not been any serious attempt to simplify or reduce the number of manufacturing operations. Given the improved level of manufacturing technology in existence as the 19th century drew to a close, compared to the labour intensive methods employed prior to the "American system" being installed at Enfield, it would seem, particularly with the benefit of 21st-century hindsight, that the War Office policy of weapon selection by competition rather than through the issue of a design brief, meant that a golden opportunity to reduce the cost of plant, equipment, measurement and inspection had been missed.

William Ellis Metford (1824–99) who designed the seven-groove barrel of the Lee Metford rifle.

EXAMINING A COCKTAIL OF COMPLEXITIES AND PROBABILITIES

In this chapter it has not been possible, through lack of substantive information, to look comprehensively through the eyes of 19th-century Ordnance observers to analyse, from their perspective, how they saw the relationship between weapon design and ease of manufacture. To date, John Anderson has been the only credible Ordnance employee found who firmly grasped these engineering concepts. Therefore, the opportunity will be taken to introduce

Rifle Lee Metford Mk II (0.45 inch) c.1892.

some possible scenarios for Ordnance, based upon 19th-century evidence while relying on 21st-century experience.

To avoid future difficulties and to ensure maximum economic benefit as manufacturing methods advanced and weapons become more complex in specification, it would have been necessary for any factory management to review the capabilities of their machinery, their production processes and workforce skills before a new product was introduced. In the 21st century these problems would tend to be addressed by integrating product design with the manufacturing process. One way to achieve this would be to establish a post-development team of engineers at the manufacturing site to act in a liaison capacity between the shop floor and the original design team. Experience has shown that without a policy or a coordinated strategy, which takes into account all the manufacturing and design aspects of a product, a factory will inevitably suffer from poor quality and delays. This will result in loss of manufacturing output and, as a consequence, a more expensive product. In the case of a private-sector company in a competitive business environment, a loss of market share could result.

One might speculate as to why the War Office did not, as the 19th century progressed, introduce or consider a coordinated design, development and production programme for weapon manufacture. This might have saved the Exchequer a considerable amount of money. Was it because Ordnance procurement and manufacture was controlled by military bureaucrats who were interested only in how the weapon performed, not in how it was made? Perhaps it was due to the fact that the Enfield factory was effectively under government control. Traditionally, such establishments have been hampered in their operations by the complexities of the decision-making process which is linked to Parliament through committees and civil servants. This prevents speed of decision making and compromises flexibility, which in turn can reduce the expected benefits derived from an economy of scale. It is known that smaller, leaner companies are often more responsive to market need, particularly if they have observed a large competitor go to the expense of pioneering a new product or process. One might cite the Birmingham Small Arms Company (BSA) as a case in point. Unlike the RSAF at Enfield, they did not at first establish all manufacturing operations under one roof. In the early years of operation not only did they employ both machine and manual methods of gun manufacture, they also put work out to local barrel makers. Presumably this was to help reduce initial set-up costs. The "spin off" effect from this would help to spread the load of the work in progress, thereby helping to cushion a rapid decline in skilled workmen within the area. In 1865, a correspondent writing in *The Engineer* said of BSA that it not only had the advantage of having "only to step into Staffordshire for its iron and it commands the best market for its stocks", but also that "conducting its business through businessmen, who cannot afford to manufacture at a loss, it possesses one other advantage which Government does not". This 19th-century notion of government manufacturing establishments not being particularly efficient and cost effective has been maintained by many, either rightly or wrongly, right up to the present day.

The lack of an integrated design and manufacturing policy may also have been a hangover from the days of the old contract system. Under this regime, government had to appease the private gun trade by allowing the bulk of the small-arms work to go to them. However, in one respect this was a benefit for government, as it allowed Ordnance to defray production costs by the arrangement of out-work, thereby keeping down expenditure on capital equipment and labour. Having such a manufacturing system in existence would have lent itself more readily to military weapon selection by open competition, albeit that the performance of the weapon eventually chosen was a compromise. In the short term, this method of selection might have appeared attractive to those controlling the government purse strings, being less costly than employing an internal weapon-design team.

Government could be forgiven if it had taken the view that the technology of the standard soldier's firearm was reaching its zenith by the final quarter of the century and development was, as a consequence, slowing down. Therefore, from a government perspective it might have seemed that there was little benefit to be gained from the expense of establishing an in-house design team, had this particular aspect been recognised. The slowing-down process can be identified most dramatically in the design of the Lee Enfield rifle. This weapon continued in British military service from the 1890s through over six decades which included two World Wars, with little alteration to the basic design.

It might be further argued that in the 19th century only a private company, free of bureaucratic control, could effectively achieve an integrated programme of product design linked to an efficient method of production. Ideally such a company would require the capability to design, although not necessarily to construct, both the product and the machine tools to produce it. Such a company would have required the confidence and financial security of long-term contracts and it was usually only the government who could provide the necessary support in terms of scale. From the evidence available, it would seem that the British government would not have been prepared to invest in such a venture, as it was content to rely mainly upon its own in-house and contractor manufacturing, while allowing weapon development to evolve through the method of open competition, trial and experiment. To date, research has only uncovered a small number of references in official documents to considerations of ease of manufacture. Occasionally a rejection is witnessed on grounds of expense and possible difficulties in producing the weapon. This happened in the case of the Owen Jones rifle during the initial technical evaluation trials in 1882, but this remains a fairly isolated case.

John Anderson, the highly regarded Ordnance engineer, when giving evidence before the 1854 Select Committee on Small Arms, on being asked the question "You are of the opinion therefore that every part of a musket is so simple as to be capable of being produced by machinery?" responded thus:

> Yes. I should mention that there are some of the present parts that have an irregular form, which have nothing to do with the musket, as a musket, neither with its accuracy or its quality, and that many of these, if I had anything to do with the getting up of the manufactory, I would prefer that they were altered in form; simplified and made more chaste in appearance, and not so crooked as some things are without any necessity.

The conclusions drawn by Anderson relating to weapon design for ease of manufacture, shortly before the installation of the American machine tools at Enfield would tend to support the theory that at least there was an early recognition in Britain of these issues by people with manufacturing backgrounds. At first this might suggest that Anderson's opinions had either been forgotten, or deliberately ignored. However, it is more likely that his views were overridden by the many complex factors, some historic, which existed just prior to the Crimean War, and which led to expediency determining the outcome for Ordnance.

Had Anderson's views been implemented, this would have meant Ordnance committing resources to employing weapon designers. These men would have had to be proficient in understanding the requirements of the latest machine tools or, at least, be engineers capable of writing detailed weapon specifications which were easy for manufacturers to comprehend and suited to contract by tender. With war looming and pressure on Ordnance to fully mechanise its manufacturing operation at Enfield, it was unlikely that options

Rifle Minié Pattern 1851, 0.702 inch. This rifle preceded the Enfield Pattern 1853 and was one of several different calibre weapons used by the British at the Crimea.

to improve weapon design to aid ease of manufacture would have been given high priority. As we have seen, Britain's entry into the Crimean War late in March 1854 coincided almost exactly with the decision to equip Enfield with the latest American machine tools, although the decision came too late for the Army to benefit from the eventual increase in weapon production. Given the state of weapon supplies at the start of the Russian conflict, it would have been irresponsible of Ordnance to have tampered with the design of the Pattern 1853. Design changes to the Pattern 1853 would have meant new sets of gauges to accommodate the simplified part profiles envisaged by Anderson. This would have led in turn to changes in inspection procedures. Not only would there have been serious consequences for future manufacturing output at Enfield had things gone wrong, but Ordnance would also have risked causing delays to the production of arms supplied by the private contractors (a major source), as it would have taken time to prepare new jigs and gauges for the private sector. As a consequence, the front-line troops at the Crimea would have been seriously prejudiced.

However, it is probably fair to conclude that the argument for leaving the design of the weapon unaltered, so as not to cause production or supply difficulties, was not generally understood by senior members of the Board of Ordnance. Research at the National Archive has provided a considerable amount of evidence, extracted from correspondence between Captain Dixon, Superintendent of the RSAF, and Viscount Hardinge (who during the Crimean conflict had been appointed General Commander in Chief of the Forces) over the latter's wish to introduce new types of arm regardless of the complexities of manufacturing and tooling-up timescales. A further reason for the Pattern 1853 remaining unaltered was that in 1852 Hardinge, then Master General of Ordnance, had been responsible for instituting a competition between small arms inventors which had led to the development of this weapon. Once this weapon had gone into production, it would have been unlikely that Hardinge would have risked a further period of experimentation with what had become the accepted service weapon. This would have been a particularly sensitive and unsettling time as the Pattern 1853 had just succeeded the short lived Minié, introduced by his predecessor the Marquis of Anglesey.

Viscount Henry Hardinge (1785–1856), Master General of Ordnance at the time of the Crimean War. Hardinge lost a left hand at the Battle of Ligny on 16 June 1815, two days before Waterloo.

There was a further important ingredient which should not be overlooked as it would have provided a distinct disincentive to making the Pattern 1853 easier to manufacture. After the death of the Duke of Wellington in 1852, it was Hardinge's decision that was ultimately responsible, through the introduction of the Pattern 1853, for reducing the calibre of the standard military weapon to 0.577 inch. This decision could have proved a potential strategic disaster for the Army. Previously British calibres tended to be in excess of 0.7 inch, as Wellington had advocated that "the English musket-ball should not be altered as a principle". He was of the opinion that the heavier calibre ball would break a horse's leg, while a lighter ball would only wound and not cripple the animal. Wellington's view was probably a throw-back from earlier wars when the use of cavalry was quite extensive. Bringing down a horse with its armed rider was an important and strategic part of warfare. As the sophistication of weapons improved, with increased range, rapidity of fire, and accuracy, the use of cavalry became less important and would eventually become obsolete. However, Hardinge could not have been absolutely sure, in the middle of the 19th century, that the introduction of the smaller calibre would bring about the advantages envisaged and the decision on his part to accept the design was probably a calculated gamble. Even if he had understood the manufacturing advantages to be gained from design modifications to the arm, it is doubtful if he would have risked further changes.

ANDERSON HAS A 20TH-CENTURY SUPPORTER

It is interesting to observe that the earlier views of John Anderson regarding ease of weapon manufacture are supported almost 80 years later by the Superintendent of the RSAF, G.H. Roberts. When writing the history of the factory in the early 1930s, whilst fully acknowledging Anderson's self-confessed lack of expertise concerning the ballistic science of small arms, Roberts is nevertheless sympathetic to his views on how a weapon might be designed to improve its ability to be manufactured. This can be seen from his comments:

> as an Engineer and Mechanic he [Anderson] was of the opinion that the designs might be very much simplified so as to make them easier and cheaper for manufacture without in any way interfering with the efficiency of the weapon – a line of

Short Magazine Lee Enfield
Rifle Mk III (0.303 inch),
introduced into service in
1907. The term 'short' refers
to the barrel length.

argument which has had to be again used by the present writer
and his staff during the last few years.

It would seem from the results of research presented above and also
by the general lack of documentary evidence concerning ease of
manufacture, particularly at times when new weapons were being
evaluated, that this feature was given a low priority on the Ordnance
scale of desirability. From the comments expressed by Roberts, it
would seem that this state of affairs persisted well into the first part
of the 20th century. Further research would be required, which is
beyond the scope of this book, to confirm how widespread the lack
of integrated design and manufacturing really was.

Because the Lee Enfield magazine rifle (in slightly modified form)
stayed so long with the British Army, it would be interesting to
discover through a future project if small arms selection had been
reduced to no more than refining the standard service weapon. If
this proved to be the case, then 19th-century selection methods
would have indelibly stamped their mark on the future of military
arms procurement. It would seem clear from the above evidence
that the main objective for 19th-century selectors of British military
arms was to ensure that the weapon chosen performed well in all
aspects of battlefield conditions and was therefore capable of
eliminating the enemy. Of course it was important for selectors to
ensure unit costs of small arms were kept to a minimum but the
predominant criterion for selection was how the
weapon performed overall. If it could be manufactured
easily and cheaply then this was a bonus.

From the evidence before us, one must conclude that,
influenced by the method of weapon selection which
had evolved in parallel with the contract system, it was
military battlefield performance which took
precedence over best engineering practice in weapon
design and manufacture, thereby delaying advances in
weapon design and manufacturing technology in
Britain.

An Afghan soldier with a Lee
Enfield Rifle c.1980. This
gives some idea of the
longevity and serviceability of
these superbly designed
weapons.

REFERENCES

Blackmore, Howard L. (1961) *British Military Firearms* (1650–1850) p.227.

Dictionary of National Biography (1908) London: Smith Elder & Co.

The Engineer, 25 March 1859, p.204, "The Royal Small-Arm Manufactory, Enfield".

> (Also see *The Mechanics Magazine*, 6 September 1861, p.145, "Leviathan Workshops No.11 the Enfield Small Arms Factory". Referring to the RSAF during production of the long Pattern 1853 Enfield, it is suggested that "upwards of 800 machines and approaching 2,000 hands – young and old are employed. 350 finished rifles per day is the maximum rate of production; and upon each rifle there are expended nearly 800 separate processes of manipulation".)

The Engineer, Vol. 19, 14 April 1865, p.224, "Gun Making by Machinery, The Small Heath Factory".

House of Lords Record Office, London, Select Committee on Small Arms, 1854, evidence of John Anderson, pp.29 and 75.

House of Lords Record Office, London, Proceedings of the Committee Appointed by the Secretary of State for War, June 1864, Reference: Accounts and Papers 1864 XXXV, p.302.

House of Lords Record Office, London, Subject: On the Conversion of the Enfield rifle to a Breech-loader, 6 February 1865, Reference: Accounts and Papers 1865 XXX11, p.355.

House of Lords Record Office, London, Subject: Mr. Snider's Method of Converting the Enfield to a Breech-loader, June 1866, Reference: Accounts and Papers 1866 XL1, p.403.

House of Lords Record Office, London, Subject: The Trials of nine descriptions of Breech-loading Rifles accepted for competition in accordance with the terms of the War Office Advertisement of 22/10/66, Reference: Reports Commissioners 1866–8, XV1, pp.32–4.

House of Lords Record Office, London, The Committees Army and Ordnance Expenditure Session, 1 Feb. – 1st Aug. 1949, Vol.9, pp.305–7.

Lumley, Roger (1989) "The American System of Manufactures in Birmingham: Production Methods at the Birmingham Small Arms Co. in the Nineteenth Century", *Business History*, Vol. 31, pp.30–1.

National Archive, Kew, Correspondence from James Aston to Master General of the School of Musketry, 21 January 1885, and letter from Harrison Trent to the Secretary of State for War, 12th January 1885, Reference Supply 5/887.

Putnam, Tim and Weinbren, Dan (1992) "A Short History of the Royal Small Arms Factory Enfield", p.38, Enfield: Middlesex University.

> (In conversation, Professor Putnam has put forward an interesting point of view, suggesting that mechanised advances in American small arms manufacture had chiefly derived benefit from its workmen, who unlike their British counterparts, had no big gun industry to distract them.)

Reynolds, E.G.B., "Enfield Arms, the early Breech-Loaders", Small Arms Profile, No.18, pp.103 and 117.

Rigby, John, "The Manufacture of Small Arms", Section.1, Minutes of Proceedings, The Institute of Civil Engineers, 29 November 1892, p.11.

Royal Armouries, Leeds, "Notes on the History of the Royal Small Arms Factory, Enfield Lock". Unsigned typed manuscript c.1930, accompanied by a memorandum, dated 24/12/30, signed G.H. Roberts, (Superintendent RSAF 1922-1931), clearly showing that he was the author of the RSAF history, p.C12.

Royal Armouries, Leeds (1852) "Report of Experiments With Small Arms, Carried on at The Royal Manufactory, Enfield".

Skentebery, Norman (1975) *Arrows to Atom Bombs, a History of the Ordnance Board*, HMSO, pp.12-14.

Smith, Merritt Roe (1977) *Harpers Ferry Armoury and the New Technology*, London: Cornell University Press, pp.219 and 249.

4. WHAT DID YOU DO IN THE WAR ALLY PALLY?

Many people know that Alexandra Palace, prominently positioned on the crest of the western slopes of the Lea Valley, is the birthplace of public service (high-definition) television broadcasting. However, what is not commonly known is the role played behind the scenes, by engineers and scientists, when television broadcasts from Alexandra Palace ceased at the start of the Second World War in September 1939.

It has generally been assumed that during the war years the transmitting equipment was mothballed or, at best, put on a care and maintenance basis. Nothing, however, could be further from the truth. The story that is about to be told concerns the wartime involvement of the scientific intelligence agencies and the highly secret world of those who worked in the field of electronic counter measures.

The original BBC television sound and vision aerials at the top of the Alexandra Palace mast. From here the signals were transmitted, during the Second World War to jam German navigational signals.

BRITAIN UNDER ATTACK

The apparent success of the German bombing raids on London and elsewhere in Britain, during the early part of the war, did not occur just because skilled navigators could find their targets by expert calculation. Even after the demolition of Bazalgette's highly ornate Moorish-style chimneys at the Abbey Mills pumping station at Stratford, thought by the authorities to be acting as landmarks for enemy aircraft, the Luftwaffe were still identifying targets in the Docks and London's East End. Bombers could also find their targets almost anywhere in Britain on nights when the weather was poor and clouds screened the ground from aerial view. Clearly it would appear that the Luftwaffe was blessed with more than its fair share of luck, or could there have been another reason for its success? To understand why the Luftwaffe was having these early successes it will first be necessary to delve into the highly secret world of intelligence gathering.

THE SECRET WORLD OF INTELLIGENCE GATHERING

It so happened that one of the last war's greatest scientific minds, the late Professor R.V. Jones, had been attached to Air Intelligence. From there he had been sent to "Station X" (this is what we now know to have been the centre of the Intelligence Services at Bletchley Park) where the German Enigma Codes were eventually broken by the mathematician Alan Turing and the teams of cryptographers. The reason for Jones being sent to Bletchley Park was to see if he could find any clues, in the pre-war files of the Secret Intelligence Service (S.I.S.) that might lead to the discovery of information relating to the existence of a secret weapon held by the Germans. Interest had been aroused when it was reported that Adolf Hitler had referred to the possibility of such a weapon during one of his speeches. After investigation, Jones concluded that there was no substance to the story and he put this down to confusion

R.V. Jones (later Professor) c.1937.

arising out of the incorrect interpretation of Hitler's speech by Foreign Office officials. However, while carrying out his research Jones reported that he had found references which suggested that the Germans were considering the development of new gases, bacterial warfare, flame weapons, gliding bombs, aerial torpedoes, pilotless aircraft, long-range guns and long-range rockets. Jones was of the opinion that all of these possible developments must be taken most seriously. Jones's early research does not appear to have uncovered anything about the success of the early bombing raids (his brief did not cover this) but, by a remarkable twist of fate, his work was to lead to some highly relevant discoveries concerning German long-range navigation.

On returning to London, Jones was asked to examine material that had just been passed to the British Naval Attaché in Oslo from an anonymous source. This turned out to be details of an electronic proximity detector for shells and a typed seven-page document, which coincidentally suggested that many of the weapons that Jones had highlighted in his report had already been developed or were undergoing development by the Germans. Also in the information received, in what became known as the "Oslo Report", it was suggested that German radar stations had detected aircraft of RAF Bomber Command at a range of 120 kilometres (80 miles) before they had carried out a raid on Wilhelmshafen. It was probably this early German technological superiority that allowed so many of the returning aircraft from the raid to be shot down on their way home. Here were the first clues that allowed the fertile mind of Jones to come up with some early opinions about the navigational abilities of German aircraft.

Interestingly, the Oslo documents also contained references to the use of radio beams, which were able to guide German bombers accurately to targets in Britain and it was this discovery, not universally believed by all in high places, that caused Jones to alert the scientific services and other intelligence agencies to his findings. He asked them to monitor carefully German radio signals and also to question closely captured aircrew. Furthermore he requested the various agencies to look for any evidence of beam receiving or transmitting equipment in shot down enemy aircraft.

THE ESTABLISHMENT OF RADIO COUNTER MEASURES

Early in 1940 the late Sir Robert Cockburn, who prior to the war had lectured at West Ham Municipal College on scientific subjects and was an expert in very high frequency radio (VHF), was moved from the Royal Aircraft Establishment at Farnborough to the Telecommunications Research Establishment (TRE) at Worth Matravers near Swanage in Dorset. His job was to set up the new Radio Counter Measures unit (RCM). There he was joined by Dr (later Professor) Ewart Farvis, from Swansea University, who soon afterwards was given the job of monitoring the German radar signals. This he did from different locations along the south coast with equipment set up in a small van. Cockburn, incidentally, was later to monitor and to analyse, with the aid of an oscilloscope, a more sophisticated German radio beam from a vantage point on Beacon Hill in Wiltshire, where a small field station had been established. It is believed that Beacon Hill had been chosen because it was due north and also in line of sight of a German radio installation at Cherbourg.

In the meantime, Jones's early suspicions of Germany's lead in navigational technology had been confirmed mainly through the work of the intelligence services. A document taken from a crashed Heinkel He 111 in March 1940 referred to "Radio beacon Knickebein from 0600 on 315 degrees". By June, Jones had been shown a decoded Enigma message by Group Captain Blandy, the head of RAF "Y" Service (a group responsible for monitoring the German radio signals) which, after translation into English, read "Kleve [Cleves the west German town] Knickebein is confirmed at position 53 degrees 24 minute North 1 degree West". From this Jones was able to explain to Blandy that Knickebein (crooked leg, after the shape of the aerial) was a German radio beam transmitter set up at Cleves and the geographic position contained within the message was a site in Britain one mile south of Retford on the Great North Road. Through the initiative of Jones, the survivors from a recently downed Heinkel He 111 that had been on a raid over the Firth of Forth were interrogated but they revealed nothing about Knickebein. However, when the prisoners were alone, one was overheard to say to the other that the British would never find the equipment they were looking for no matter how hard they tried. When Jones received this information, along with a technical report on the crashed aircraft, his suspicions were immediately aroused and he telephoned the Royal Aircraft Establishment at Farnborough and spoke to the scientist who had carried out the investigation on the crashed Heinkel. From the conversation he learned that the only unusual thing that could be found was the high sensitivity of the radio equipment used for blind landing. The system of blind landing, known as Lorenz, had been in operation with civil airlines before the war and was typically functional five miles from an airport. Lorenz worked on the principle that the pilot flew down the centre of a radio beam, which comprised different signals on either side (dots and dashes). If the pilot was on course he heard a continuous note in his headphones, but if he veered off track to either the left or right the note would change until he returned to the correct heading. Obviously, the presence of a receiver with a

A diagram showing an aircraft flying in the 'steady note' zone of the Lorenz Beam blind landing system.

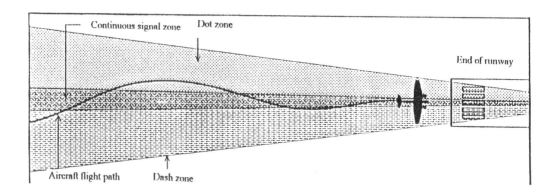

Continuous signal zone   Dot zone

End of runway

Aircraft flight path   Dash zone

range beyond five miles (probably as much as 200) was, for Jones, a dead giveaway.

THAT "EUREKA" MOMENT

However, understanding how an aircraft could be made to fly in a straight line was one thing; but how did the aircrew determine the distance (range) so that they would know when to release their bombs precisely on target? Jones was convinced that there had to be a second beam that would intersect with the first to accurately pinpoint range. As luck would have it, the intelligence services found the answer on a piece of paper recovered from a German aircraft shot down in France which gave the location of the second transmitter as Schleswig Holstein. Further confirmation was gained when material was collected from other downed enemy aircraft and also through the interrogation of a German prisoner. These discoveries provided the British scientists with sufficient information on the working of Knickebein (two-beam system with a transmitter frequency of 30 MHz) to allow the team of Cockburn and Farvis to begin in earnest the design of equipment that would effectively jam it. A second improved navigational system, known as X-Gerät (X-Apparatus), with a ranging accuracy of about 450 metres (Knickebein was accurate to around 1,500 metres) had also been detected by TRE. This second system also used two intersecting beams to determine range but was on a higher frequency of 70 MHz. Quite remarkably, by Christmas 1940, TRE had designed equipment to jam both X-Gerät and Knickebein.

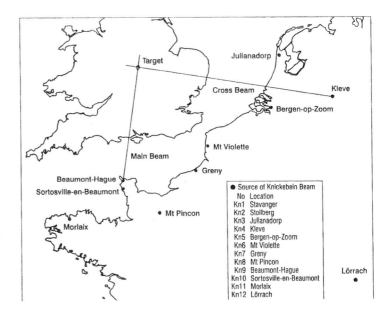

Map showing the cross beam Knickebein navigation system. Where the beams crossed was the point where the air crew released their bomb load.

THE GERMANS BECOME MORE SOPHISTICATED

In the meantime German scientists had been working on a third navigational aid called Y-Gerät, which was considerably more sophisticated than the earlier two systems. Y-Gerät did not rely on finding the target by the method of two intersecting beams but used a 300–3,000 Hz signal superimposed (modulated) on a 42 MHz carrier wave transmitted by a ground station (in this case Cassel near Calais), which when picked up by the aircraft's radio receiver was re-transmitted back to the sending station on the ground at a higher frequency of 45 MHz. Due to a phase delay (caused by the time taken by the signal to travel out and back) between the transmitted and returned signals, which the operator at the ground station could measure, it was possible to calculate the position of the aircraft along the beam and therefore the distance. Using this information, in conjunction with a good scale map on which the geographical position of the target had first been selected, it was possible to position the aircraft correctly over the bombing zone. A further co-sited transmitter with a carrier frequency of 43.5 MHz sent a series of equal left and right pulses, using a principle not too dissimilar from Lorenz (described earlier), although in this instance not as dots and dashes. The signal information from the ground was processed by the airborne equipment and fed to a display meter with a centre zero needle. To maintain the aircraft's correct heading the pilot had to ensure that the needle remained central within the display. When the ground station had calculated that the pilot was correctly positioned over the target a radiotelegraphy (R/T) message was sent instructing him to release his bombs. This system of navigation was said to have accuracy to within 275 metres of the target.

The German scientists had become aware that the British had found a way to jam successfully both X-Gerät and Knickebein so the Y-Gerät system was speedily put into operation. As it transpired, the speed with which German scientists had made the system

An X-beam transmitter (Wotan I).

A series of cartoons drawn by the BBC engineer Wilf Pafford (Paff) during his wartime service at Alexandra Palace.

operational would prove extremely helpful to British counter measures. It had been noticed during monitoring by some quick-thinking person in Cockburn's team that Y-Gerät was working within the same frequency spectrum (40–50 MHz) as the sound and vision television transmitters at Alexandra Palace. Clearly, this was a tactical error on behalf of the German scientists, but a brilliant stroke of luck for their British counterparts.

ALLY PALLY JOINS THE WAR

During the early part of the war, Tony Bridgewater, a senior BBC engineer, had been instructed to get the Alexandra Palace transmitters up and running on a care and maintenance basis (he probably did not know why he was doing this). At the time, British Intelligence had received information that Germany was planning a seaborne invasion of Britain (Operation Sealion) and it was thought that the Alexandra Palace transmitter could be used to jam German radio communications. Once the transmitter had been brought back to life and was running correctly, Bridgewater volunteered to join the armed forces. In about October 1940, the task of maintaining the transmitter was handed to another BBC engineer, Wilf Pafford, renowned for his amusing "Paff" cartoons. Pafford was to remain as engineer in charge at Alexandra Palace for the duration of the war.

During the following weeks other engineers were drafted to Alexandra Palace where they carried out modifications to the transmitter so that it could be re-tuned quickly. They also carried out work to allow the transmitter to be switched from standby to

A Heinkel III fitted with X-beam receiving antennae.

full power by remote control. Farvis was sent from TRE to set up a listening post and control centre, which he did at a BBC out-station at Swains Lane, Highgate. Once there, in a true engineering spirit of make-do-and-mend, he arranged for a domestic pre-war EMI television receiver to be modified to receive R/T signals and other relevant transmissions within the range of 40–50 MHz. This was to enable engineers to listen to radio instructions sent from the German ground stations at Cassel and elsewhere on the Continent to the navigators on bombing raids over Britain. The modified television receiver also monitored the superimposed frequencies on the Y-Gerät radio beam of both the ground station and the aircraft.

Swains Lane had been chosen to be a listening and monitoring post as it was a BBC cable centre close to Alexandra Palace. In the early days of outside broadcasts, Swains Lane had been used, rather like a telephone exchange, to link television pictures and sound signals from fixed points around London to Alexandra Palace via landlines (this was before the days of microwave and satellite links).

Having the direct cable links to Alexandra Palace meant that engineers at Swains Lane could listen to the German radio messages and, at the appropriate moment, bring the transmitter out of stand-by through a method of remote control via landline. It was also possible, through a remotely controlled motor drive unit at Alexandra Palace, to re-tune the transmitter to match the frequency of the German signals should they be changed. To make sure that all the modifications were carried out swiftly, engineers worked a shift system around the clock. By 4th February 1941 everything was in place for Alexandra Palace to become the first known almost undetectable jamming station. By an extraordinary piece of luck, 4 February 1941 was also the date of the first raid on Britain using Y-Gerät.

JAMMING ENEMY COMMUNICATIONS
The method devised to jam the Y-Gerät signal was simplicity itself. Farvis and his team received and monitored the incoming beam signal from Cassel (the one which gave the aircraft direction) and they would then pass this "captured" frequency via landline to Alexandra Palace. There it would be superimposed (modulated) onto the 45 MHz carrier wave generated by the television transmitter, which had been adjusted to match the frequency of the aircraft's return transmission to Cassel. However, the modulated frequency fed by landline from Swains Lane to Alexandra Palace was slightly out of phase, due to the time delay between the two sites. This created a "howl round" effect when the transmitter was

switched on and can be likened to the noise from a public address system when the microphone amplifier is turned up too high, only in this instance the results were at radio frequency (R/F), rather than audio frequency (A/F). The trick was for Swains Lane to listen carefully to the instructions being sent to the navigator from Cassel and then to remotely switch on the transmitter at Alexandra Palace a few seconds before the bomb release message could be received by the aircraft. When Swains Lane had decided that the navigator had missed his opportunity to identify the target, the Alexandra Palace transmitter would be returned to standby mode as the aircraft returned to base without releasing its bombs. It has been claimed that only about 25 per cent of all Y-Gerät controlled missions released their bomb loads. The German Y-Gerät raids persisted until late May 1941 without altering any of the carrier-wave frequencies, which would suggest that the British counter measures had not been detected. However, after this, the frequencies were regularly changed; but thanks to the foresight of Farvis and his team, it was a simple matter to re-tune the Alexandra Palace transmitter quickly.

The BBC vision transmitter and control desk at Alexandra Palace c.1949.

I have been told by a BBC engineer that the people who were monitoring the radio communication between Cassel and the aircraft, at the point when the Alexandra Palace transmitter was turned on, fell about laughing as the bomber's navigator accused the scientists at the German ground station of supplying useless equipment while the ground station controller accused the navigator of being incompetent in his operation. So it would appear that there was a little light relief during Britain's darkest hour.

All of us today owe a great debt of gratitude to the TRE counter-measure boffins and the BBC engineers who, through their scientific skills, were able to prevent a greater loss of life and injury than actually occurred. All of this could not have been achieved without the assistance of the BBC's television transmitter and mast at Alexandra Palace, Wood Green, the latter now surmounted with aerials that provide the latest Digital Audio Broadcast (DAB) technology. Perhaps when next glancing at the familiar mast silhouetted against the skyline on the western ridge of the Lea Valley, a thought can be spared for its wartime role.

REFERENCES

Alexander, Robert Charles (1999) *The Life and Works of Alan Dower Blumlein*, Oxford: Focal Press.

Brettingham, Laurie (1997) *Royal Air Force Beam Benders No. 80 (Signals) Wing, 1940-1945*, Midland Publishing Limited.

Gray, Jack, "Alexandra Palace – Battle of the Beams (1940-1941)", *BBC Engineering Information* No. 51, Winter 1992/3.

Gray, Jack, Interview, October 2000.

Jones, Reginald Victor (1998) *Most Secret War*, Hertfordshire: Wordsworth Editions Limited.

Note 1

The author is indebted to Jack Gray, a former BBC engineer who had personally interviewed Professor R.V. Jones, Sir Robert Cockburn, Tony Bridgewater, W.C. Pafford and Professor Ewart Farvis, and generously passed on his research notes to make this chapter possible. Also the author would like to acknowledge the help received from Laurie Brettingham and the kind permission to reproduce diagrams from his book.

Note 2

Due to the relative complexity of the Lorenz, X-Gerät, Y-Gerät and Knickebein systems, the author has endeavoured to explain their working without too much technical jargon. However, should the reader require a fuller treatment, it is recommended that publications in the list of references are consulted.

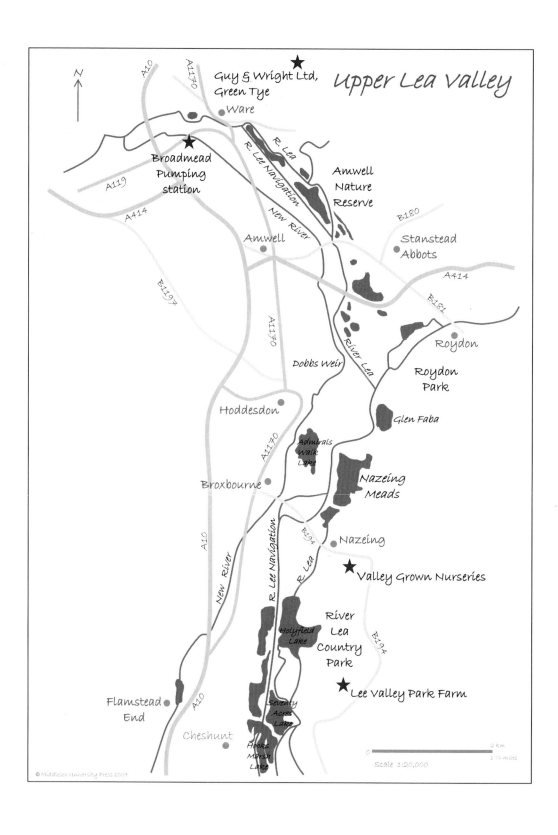

Upper Lea Valley

N

★ Guy & Wright Ltd, Green Tye

● Ware

★ Broadmead Pumping station

R. Lee Navigation

R. Lea

New River

A10
A1170
A119
A414
B1197
A1170

● Amwell

Amwell Nature Reserve

B180

Stanstead Abbots ●

A414

B181

Dobbs Weir

River Lea

Roydon ●

Roydon Park

Glen Faba

● Hoddesdon

Admirals Walk Lake

Nazeing Meads

A1170

● Broxbourne

B194

Nazeing ●

★ Valley Grown Nurseries

R. Lee Navigation

R. Lea

New River

A10

R. Lee Navigation

River Lea Country Park

Holyfield Lake

B194

★ Lee Valley Park Farm

Flamstead End ●

A10

Cheshunt ●

Seventy Acres Lake

Hooks Marsh Lake

0   2 km
                 1 ¼ miles
Scale 1:20,000

© Middlesex University Press 2009

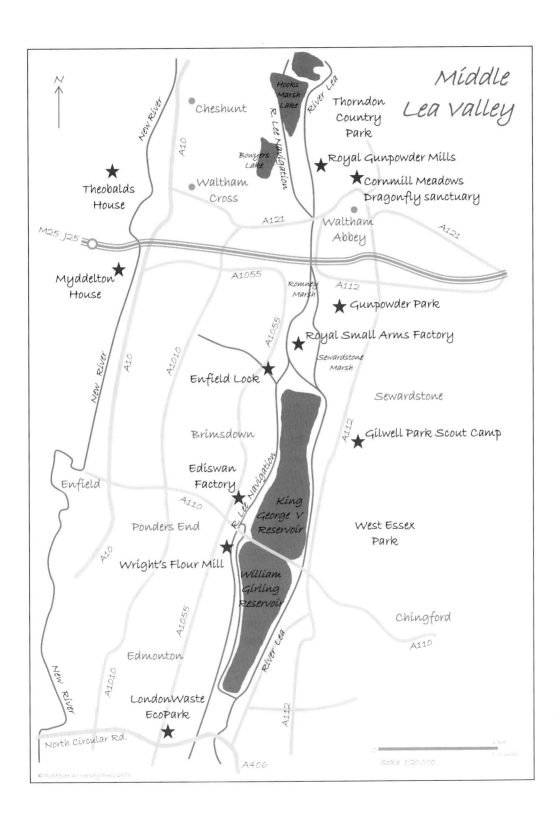

Middle Lea Valley

N

New River

Cheshunt

Hooks Marsh Lake

River Lea

Thorndon Country Park

R. Lee Navigation

Bowyers Lake

A10

★ Royal Gunpowder Mills

★ Cornmill Meadows Dragonfly sanctuary

★ Theobalds House

Waltham Cross

A121

Waltham Abbey

A121

M25 J25

★ Myddelton House

A1055

Romney Marsh

A112

★ Gunpowder Park

New River

A10

A1010

A1055

★ Royal Small Arms Factory

Sewardstone Marsh

★ Enfield Lock

Brimsdown

Sewardstone

A112

★ Gilwell Park Scout Camp

Ediswan Factory

Lee Navigation

★

King George V Reservoir

West Essex Park

Enfield

A110

Ponders End

Ri

★ Wright's Flour Mill

A10

William Girling Reservoir

Chingford

A110

A1055

Edmonton

New River

A1010

River Lea

★ LondonWaste EcoPark

A112

North Circular Rd.

A406

Scale 1:20,000

© Middlesex University Press 2009

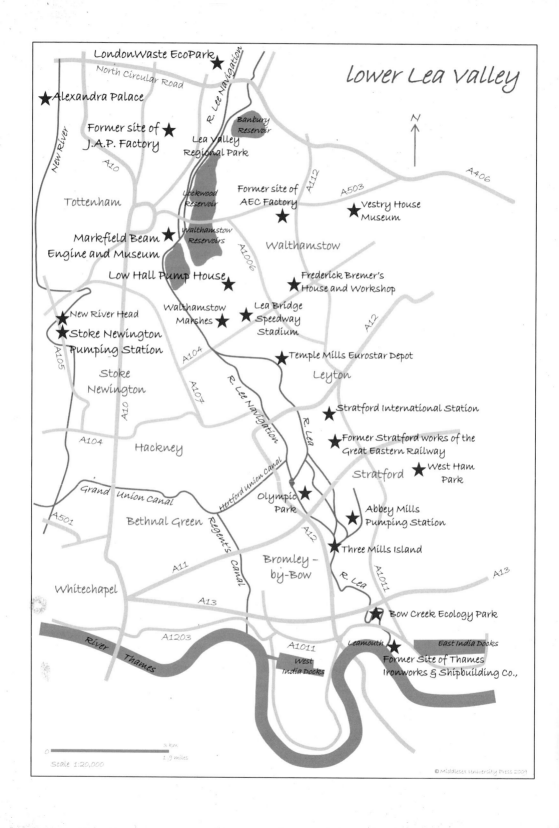

Lower Lea Valley

LondonWaste EcoPark
North Circular Road
R. Lee Navigation
Banbury Reservoir

Alexandra Palace

Former site of
J.A.P. Factory
Lea Valley Regional Park

New River
A10

Tottenham

Lockwood Reservoir

Former site of AEC Factory

A112
A503

Vestry House Museum

A406

N

Markfield Beam Engine and Museum
Walthamstow Reservoirs

Walthamstow
A1006

Low Hall Pump House

Frederick Bremer's House and Workshop

New River Head
Stoke Newington Pumping Station

A105

Walthamstow Marshes

Lea Bridge Speedway Stadium

A12

Stoke Newington

A104
A107

R. Lee Navigation

Temple Mills Eurostar Depot

Leyton

R. Lea

Hackney

A104

Stratford International Station

Former Stratford works of the Great Eastern Railway

A10

Grand Union Canal

Hertford Union Canal

Olympic Park

Stratford

West Ham Park

A501

Bethnal Green

Regent's Canal

Abbey Mills Pumping Station

A11

Bromley - by-Bow

A12

Three Mills Island

Whitechapel

A13

R. Lea

A1011

A13

Bow Creek Ecology Park

A1203
River Thames

A1011

Leamouth

East India Docks

West India Docks

Former Site of Thames Ironworks & Shipbuilding Co.,

0   3 km
         1.9 miles
Scale 1:20,000

© Middlesex University Press 2009